# R.E.A.C.H.

## How to Reach People Across Cultures so They Can Reach Their Potential

## MANNY **SCOTT**

PAGE TURNER PUBLISHING
ATLANTA, GA

*Design by Signify*
Library of Congress Cataloging-in-Publication Data

Scott, Manny
R.E.A.C.H. – 3rd ed.

ISBN-13: 9781790680153

# DEDICATION

I dedicate this book to every person who has a burden to help the least, the last, the lost, and the left out.

# R.E.A.C.H.

# **TABLE OF CONTENTS**

# R.E.A.C.H.

# INTRODUCTION

INTRODUCTION

After I had finished hugging, encouraging, and taking selfies with hundreds of students, a young man, with sagging pants, tattoos on his face, and a bandana hanging out of his pocket, slowly approached me. He wasn't smiling, he wasn't looking for an autograph, and he certainly wasn't interested in taking a selfie with me. He apparently had something else in mind. With each step he took toward me, he stared straight into my eyes with a look that I had seen many times in my life. In that young man's eyes was the same hardened look that I saw among gang members and drug dealers when I was growing up on the east side of Long Beach, California. He had in his eyes the same look that I've seen in prisons among people who have been convicted of rape, violence, and murder. It is a penetrating, piercing look that searches another person's soul for any hint of weakness, phoniness, or fear.

As he approached, I noticed that he had tattoos on his neck, on his knuckles, and some scars on his hands. I greeted him, but he didn't respond verbally. He just nodded his head. Without saying a word, he handed me a big, 8 x 11-inch, yellow envelope, and just stood there.

Curious, I looked down at it, and then looked back up at him, thinking he was going to say something about it, or tell me to open it or something. Nope. Still nothing. He was silent. So I looked back down at the envelope and flipped it over. On it was a drawing. It was a drawing of an open, upward-facing hand. In the palm of the hand was a candle, and at the top of the candle was a flickering flame. Around the wrist was a hand-cuff or a chain.

"This is very nice! You drew this?" I asked him.

He nodded, and then said, quietly, "yep."

I told him how nice it was and then asked him if he wanted to be an artist for a living. He just shrugged his shoulders, indicating that he wasn't sure what he wanted to be.

I then made the question more broad to see what kind of ambitions, goals, or dreams he had. "What do you want to do with your life? What do you want to be? If money weren't an issue, what would you do for free because you loved doing it so much?"

Again, he just shrugged his shoulders, and then he looked down. I sensed that my questions hit a nerve in him. I didn't want to upset him, but I wasn't in the mood to spend the rest of my afternoon trying to read his mind. "He walked up to me for a reason. Obviously, he must want to say something to me," I told myself. Still, I started to get a little impatient and tried a more direct approach. "What does this drawing mean? Why did you draw it, and why did you give it to me?"

He looked up at me for a moment and then dropped his head. I could tell that he went somewhere mentally, and he was debating whether he was going to tell me what he was thinking. He then looked up at me with a very intense, pained look in his eyes. He took a small step closer me. He was now about 10 inches from my face. What he said next broke my heart.

He said, "When I was little … my mom sold me to drug dealers … They raped me … and they raped me … and they hurt me." Tears started to well up in his eyes. He continued, "… and when they were done with me … they threw me in a dumpster … to die …" His voice was quietly trembling with pain. "But my brother found me," he said, pointing to his brother, who was standing in the distance against a wall, sobbing. Still pointing at his brother, "He found me … and he raised me … He's all I got … We're all we got." Tears started to well up in my eyes as I stood there in silence. Just listening.

He then grabbed the yellow envelope out of my hand. "This hand," he said, pointing at the hand in the drawing, "is my hand … and that candle is my hope." The volume of his voice began to rise with each phrase … "I hope that my life can get better … my hope that I can be successful … that I can be somebody." Then he paused long enough to let all the emotion that had been bottled up inside him—an emotion that he had never verbalized.

He then pointed at the handcuff or chain, and said, "But this chain lets me know that I ain't gonna be sh!#," as tears began to roll down his cheek. He repeated himself, "I ain't gonna be sh!#. I ain't gonna be shi!# … I wanna be something too." Before I could respond, I could tell he wasn't done. "I ain't gonna be sh!#." The pain was now pouring from his eyes, down his face, falling from his chin. His voice got softer, and I could almost see a little boy crying out for help. With almost a whimper, he said, "I wanna be something too … I wanna be somebody. But look at me. You know, I ain't gonna be sh!#."

How do you reach that young man, and other hopeless people, young or old, like him? How do you help someone who feels hopeless and worthless? How do you help people see that they do not have to be defined by their circumstances? How do you help people see that they matter, that they are important, and that they can overcome their obstacles to succeed in school, and graduate prepared for work and life?

I have been to forty-nine states and five continents, to huge urban areas and quiet, rural ones. Hopeless people are everywhere. They are white, black, latino, or Asian. They are rich, middle-middle class, or poor. They come from two-parent homes and single-parent homes. Sadly, many of them are drowning in despair, being suffocated by anguish, and groping for any bit of hope they can find. They are probably about to hurt themselves or others. They might be about to make a mistake that could ruin their lives or the lives of others. Some of them have knives. Some of them have guns. Some of them have hate and rage in their hearts. My friend, they need our help. They need our hope. They need to be reached.

To "reach" someone means to make a connection with that person in a way that results in them making positive mental, emotional, or behavioral changes in their lives. How can we help others do that? What kinds of things can we do to affect those kinds of positive changes in peoples' lives?

How can we you help someone who is living beneath his potential to living up to his potential? How can you reach that student who is underperforming become an honor-roll student? How can you reach that person who is living at average levels, not making the most of life? How can you reach young men and women who have bad grades, who are talking back in class, who are disrespectful, and who are apathetic about the struggles and the realities of other people? How can you reach people who are doing things in the streets or at work that are self-sabotaging and self-defeating? How do we reach people who are going down a path that is almost certainly going to lead to misery?

This book is my most complete attempt to answer those questions.

Since 2001, I have been on the road up to 200 days a year, speaking primarily at conventions, conferences, and schools to over two million administrators, teachers, leaders, and students. Roughly half of those audiences have consisted of middle and high school students. In the urban contexts, the students who were primarily Caucasian-American, African-American, and Mexican-American. The majority of them were living at or below the poverty line, and nearly all of them attended schools that were having a hard time reaching and teaching them.

To the delight of many school districts, my team and I have been able to reach many people in quite meaningful ways. For example, not too long ago, a state superintendent of public education invited me to speak in a rural school district to about 2,000 middle and high school students. During that one hour, while I was speaking at the assembly, I sensed something special happening in the room. After I finished speaking, I never have time to—and, to be quite frank, I am not even remotely interested in trying to—formally collect qualitative or quantitative data to substantiate the effectiveness of my work. Instead, after my presentations, I usually spend the bulk of my time talking one-on-one with students or audience members. It is during those moments when I try to encourage and counsel them and give them advice or direction.

Interestingly enough, I returned to that school district one year later to facilitate leadership development workshops for the district's teachers and counselors. During those sessions, one of the counselors who had attended the assembly at which I spoke the year before told me that, as a result of my presentation at the assembly, forty-three students went to counselors to seek help, because they had been thinking about committing suicide. My assembly helped students feel safe enough to admit that they needed help. Who knows how many suicides were prevented from that one assembly? How does one even begin to place a value on saving even one life? What about forty-three lives? These kinds of stories fill my heart and renew my fire to keep reaching others as long as I can.

Through the years, I have come to see more clearly the need for organizations like mine to enter into public schools and try to do holistic work with the young people. This kind of work goes against the grain of the high-stakes testing movement going on in our country. Through keynotes, seminars, and assemblies, my team and I are being used to prevent suicides, giving people hope and practical help; and, letting them know that they are loved. We are helping them see that they have the power to overcome every obstacle in their lives to achieve their dreams. We are helping them see that they can heal from the pain, or at least learn to live functional lives with the pain. Through our work, we are treating people with dignity, identifying crisis situations, and connecting people with resources that can help them flourish or fly.

As a result of our work through, test scores usually do improve. However, to be honest, test scores are the least of my concerns. I'm convinced that if we address the deeper, more fundamental issues people are facing, then their grades and lives will naturally improve.

Sadly, despite the effectiveness of our work with young people, some school leaders still refuse to hire me unless we give them "data" to demonstrate that my work actually raises test scores. Understandably, they need something to justify them investing in us. I absolutely understand that. However, in my view, the great tragedy is that their criteria for success n school is often so narrow and truncated that it disregards the most fundamental aspects of education—the development and flourishing of the whole child. But how does one quantify hope being reborn, lives being saved, and families being restored? Too many schools have no place for those kinds of measurements, to the detriment of kids, families, and communities.

Nonetheless, I am on a mission to help change that, and I am so grateful for all those leaders in education, non-profits, and corporate businesses who are partnering with me to help their students, staff, and communities flourish. They believe in me, my work, and see with enthusiasm the amazing, life-changing results that are flowing from my time with their groups.

I am seeing kids who were once thinking about dropping out of high school go to college. I have seen young people who were getting Fs and Ds turn things around academically. I have seen people who have been molested who are now seeing themselves as survivors, living each day with more zest and purpose. I am seeing young people come to me with tears in their eyes telling me that they are no longer going to cut themselves, no longer going to disrespect teachers, or dishonor their parents. I've seen real, amazing, wonderful changes take place in peoples' lives, and I am so very grateful to have played a small part in their transformations.

This book is my attempt to help people have that kind of impact on others, especially young people. If you help a young person make some decisions and develop healthy habits, you could position that young person to flourish in powerful ways. Having said that, I believe the things I share in this book can be useful with most people you meet. I will be the first to tell you that I have failed miserably time and time again when trying to reach people. But I've also been very effective in my work with others.

In this book, I want to share the things that I've seen work so that you can use them with the people that you serve. Wherever you are, wherever you work, whatever your title, whatever your position, whatever you get paid, I have no doubt that you can use the things in this book. I know that the things I share in this book work. I have used the strategies I share in this book in schools, at big corporate events, in churches, and on street corners.

Although I have no problem analyzing theories, claims, data, I'm not interested in just sharing abstract theories with you. I want to share practical things with you that you can begin using as soon as you put down this book. There are enough people writing books on theory. Quite frankly, I doubt many authors could do with your group what they recommend you should do. Unlike them, I actually use the things I share in this book.

Why have I been able to reach people across race, ethnicity, age, class, region, dialect, gender, and sexual orientation? More importantly, how can you reach more people too? That's what I will try to answer in the remainder of this book. In this book, I am going to do my best to share with you my philosophy, values, and strategies for reaching people. I'm going to share with you an approach about which I have thought long and hard. It is an approach I have been developing through the years, and this is the first time I have actually tried to put it down in writing so thoroughly. To be sure, it is a work in progress. The REACH approach is not a formula. It is not some kind of silver bullet that can reach every single person you meet. Instead, it is just one approach that I have seen have amazing results in affecting positive changes in the lives of others.

I've worked with people in some challenging places, and have learned much of what I share in this book the hard way. I have walked into thousands of rooms in nearly every major city in the United States, and I have done my best to build a bridge into the lives of my audiences. Sometimes it has gone well, and sometimes things have not. After leaving those schools, jails, conferences, or wherever I have just been, I have sometimes just sat in my car to reflect. During those times of reflection, I usually asked myself, "What worked? What didn't work? Why did that work so well? Why did they not respond to that in the way I had hoped? Why did that exercise work with the group yesterday, but did not work so well with the group today?

Then, after guessing at some answers, or discovering the need to ask more questions, I have dusted myself off, got up and tried something else during my next speaking engagement. Whether things go well or poorly, I have self-reflected, and committed to trying something else until something works.

I have noticed, for example, that some things that work with people in the Rio Grande Valley of Texas do not work in the same way with people in Dallastown, Pennsylvania. Some of what works in Arizona does not have the same impact on some people in Florida. However, with all the diversity of the United States and around the world, I have noticed some patterns of things that work in general. It's those things that I share with you in this book.

# Intended Audience of This Book

Although I am working on my doctorate in Intercultural Studies, this book is not for the academy. I am too busy right now, speaking around the country and preparing for comprehensive exams to write this book for the academy. While I might one day be sitting in an ivory tower, right now I am still working with people in the trenches. This book is for those in the trenches. It is for people who are on the front line, in the heat of battle, fighting for the hearts and minds of people who need hope and help.

Having said that, my work with real people, who have had real issues, has been my "research." My research question, in a broad sense, has been, "how can we reach people across cultural, linguistic, ethnic, racial, gender, political, socioeconomic, and religious lines so they can flourish in school, work, and life?"

In addition to all of the books I have read about this subject, the people—superintendents, teachers, CEOs, students, food service workers, paraprofessionals, parents, prisoners, and others—with whom I've worked have been my "literature review."

Also, my being on the road up to three-hundred days a year for the last two decades of my life, speaking to, and working with, people, and interviewing them informally has been my "methodology" to gather my data.

Furthermore, the students, teachers, parents, inmates, gang members, drug addicts, and others whom I have served have been my "units of analysis" or my "data." I have been "proximate" with them, spending countless hours with them, hearing their stories firsthand, crying with them, encouraging them, and empowering them to overcome some of their obstacles to reach their potential.

In that sense, the claims and arguments I make in this book are based on my critical reflections from my on-the-ground work with real people. The real human beings with whom I have worked are my evidence, my warrants, and serve as the "backing" of my claims. They satisfy the "prerequisite conditions" of my assertions.

Finally, this book is not only my "argument of discovery," but also my "argument of advocacy." It is my answer to my research question, "how can we reach people across cultural, linguistic, ethnic, racial, gender, political, socioeconomic, and religious lines so they can flourish in school, work, and life?"

Based on what I have learned on the road over these last twenty years about reaching others, I strongly urge you to understand the ideas and apply the principles and strategies I share in this book.

One day I might try to conduct formal research on this topic to gather empirical data, synthesize it, and present it to the academy in an acceptable, scholarly way, so that corporations, colleges and universities, teacher-training programs, seminaries, and other organizations can improve the ways they help people.

Interestingly enough, it is not uncommon for teachers, police officers, entrepreneurs, ministers, and others to come up to me after my presentations or seminars, and, with gratitude, tell me they learned more from me in an hour or a day than they learned in all their years of professional development or school. One teacher said, with tears in her eyes, "Manny, I learned more from you in this one hour than I learned in all my years in college or graduate school. You are an entire teacher-training curriculum! You are culturally-responsive, student-centered pedagogy embodied!" My friend, those kinds of compliments humble me because all I have wanted to do over these last twenty years was help people who were hurting and hopeless. Still, compliments like those are icing on my cake. They are sweet to my soul!

In this book, I have, for the first time, synthesized all of my personal experiences, my formal education, and my work with over two million people to create a comprehensive approach to helping people.

# Outline of This Book

In chapter one, I give you a glimpse into the life of someone who was considered "unreachable." I try to help you see life through the eyes of someone who might be very much like some of the people you would like to reach. In that chapter, I ask you two of the most critical questions you need to answer about helping others. Your answer to those questions will help you determine if your heart and mind are in the right place to continue on the path of reaching others.

In chapter two, I will introduce you to the mental map around which I frame much of the R.E.A.C.H. approach. I have a background in Rhetoric and Communication, Theology, Missiology, and Intercultural Studies, and want to share with you something that I believe can help improve your communication skills across cultures immediately. Most importantly, the diagram I share in that chapter will also serve as basis, and provide the outline for the rest of the book.

In chapters three through eleven, I spend considerable time helping you get very clear about your own frame of reference. In those chapters, I help you to examine your own frame of reference, and the frame(s) of reference of your intended audience(s). Only once you have understood yourself as well as the person you are trying to reach, can you formulate outcomes you would like them to help them achieve. That is, only after you understand people is it appropriate to begin thinking about strategies to help them.

In chapter twelve, I talk about an experience that forced me to think more critically about the concept of race and ethnicity. Race and ethnicity are not synonyms and should not be used interchangably. I explain the distinction and examine the concept of race in more depth. In our globalized, racialized world in which you must interact with people who are racially or ethnically different from you, it is vital that you think critically about race and ethnicity. That chapter will help you do that.

In chapters thirteen through eighteen, I introduce you to the R.E.A.C.H. approach that I have been developing over the last twenty years.

In a nutshell, that is what this book is about. As you read through it, really slow down, and think about how these ideas, principles, and strategies can be applied to your own context. Doing so will help you become a much more effective leader, speaker, teacher, and person.

I thank you in advance for your grace as you read this book. I might not say some things as effectively as they can be said, but I've done my best to put into words ideas that have been stirring in my head and heart for the last twenty years. If something does not make sense to you or is not very clear to you, please try to listen for my heart behind my words.

One more thing before we begin. Sometimes I say this to my live audiences, but I want to say it to you now: as you are reading this book, if something pricks you, stop and think about it. If something causes a light bulb to go off in your head, stop reading, pull out your journal or computer and write. You could even write in this book's margins. That is normally what I do.

In any case, slowly digest the things I share. Doing so will be more useful to you in the long run. Don't just rush through this book to say you finished it. Doing that will limit this book's usefulness for you. Working to understand the ideas, principles, and approach I lay out in this book will take time. It has taken me a lifetime to learn them; don't feel pressure to learn them all at once. To be frank with you, I'm still working on several of the things in this book myself. I hope to never stop working on them because I want to keep growing and increasing my impact. One thing I have found, though, is that the better I get at practicing the things I share in this book, the more significant my impact. I believe the same will be true for you too if you slow down and reflect on the things I share.

In any case, I humbly request that put your head and heart into reading this book. If you do, I believe you will begin to see some real breakthroughs in your life and in the lives of the people you hope to help.

—Manny Scott

# R.E.A.C.H.

# PART 1

## FOUNDATION

# FOUNDATION

**I**N THIS FIRST PART OF THIS BOOK, we are going to look very carefully at who you are and what you bring to every encounter you have with others. If you are going to be maximally effective at reaching people, then I think you would be very wise to begin your quest by taking an inward look at yourself.

Sometimes teachers, speakers, or leaders want to try to read their audiences to tailor their lessons or presentations to fit their audiences. As important as that is, that approach assumes that the real challenges to helping others are outside of the teacher, speaker, or leader and can be met by developing new understandings of others. However, I believe that much of your effectiveness as a teacher, speaker, or leader must begin with an examination of yourself. Even though the ultimate goal of effective cross-cultural teaching, speaking, and leading is to help people, your effectiveness must begin with an inward look rather than an outward one.

This is important because, as a teacher, speaker, or leader, you are predominantly an interpreter. You were born into a world that is interpreted and interpreting. Those interpretations shape you. So whether or not you are consciously aware of it, you have experiences that affect how you see, hear, think, and feel; and, you have frameworks of meaning that have been handed down to you from others. Those frameworks predispose how you understand yourself, others, and the world. Those frameworks also influence the kind of lessons or topics you select (and ignore) to address, the illustrations you use, the stories you tell, the language and phrases you use, the ways you apply truth, and the overall choices you make in preparing and delivering your lessons or speeches.

In short, you are not a blank slate but are inescapably conditioned by several elements. In part one of this book, we will spend a good deal of time helping you become aware of those elements.

However, just before we do that, I want to tell you about a person who needed to be reached: **me**.

————

# CHAPTER **ONE**

# UNREACHABLE?

I was once considered unreachable. I was born into a beautiful, but very broken, family. My father was in prison for most of my life. My stepfather, who was generally a good man, was an alcoholic, and he was, at one point, addicted to cocaine. There were many nights when my stepfather got so drunk or high that he physically abused my mother. I'll never forget the night that my stepfather grabbed my mother by the back of her head and slammed her face through a glass window. As a little boy, I literally had to fight for my mother's life. There were nights when I would hear my mother screaming for help and all I could do was call the police and beg them to come and save my mother.

My mother, who came from a very broken family herself, tried to find stability for us. She did the best she could with what she had been given. Nonetheless, before I was 16 years old, I had already lived in 26 places—not including the cars, the beaches, the alleys, the hotels, the motels, the homeless shelters, and all the other places we stayed. I lost count of the number of places we slept before I was 16 years old.

There were nights that we would stop at a homeless shelter because we didn't have anywhere else to go. In those shelters, I would be lying on the floor with no pillow, no blanket, and no mattress; and, I was clutching a piece of brown, stale bread, wondering why we had to sleep in places like that. As a little boy, my mind did not understand why we couldn't just call family or someone else to help us.

I remember my mother taking off her jacket, laying it over the top of me, and softly saying to me, "baby, everything's gonna be okay."

As much as I wanted to believe my mother, things were not okay. There were some nights when I would be so hungry that I would jump into dumpsters at Taco Bell, McDonald's, or some other restaurant, tear open bags, and sift through garbage, just to find something to help me make it through the night.

I was the kid that you saw coming from a block away who made you so nervous that you crossed the street. I was the kid with whom your parents refused to let you play. And, I was the kid who took all those issues with me to school.

I used to sit in class with holes in my pants, holes in my shoes, and holes in my self-esteem. While teachers assiduously covered their lesson-plans for the day, I was sitting in class thinking about the fight I had the night before against a grown man. Teachers would be covering their lesson-plans while I was sitting in my seat with sore ribs because I had recently been thrown off of a balcony. Teachers used to cover their content while I sat in their classes with my stomach growling, wondering when and where I was going to get my next meal.

In one of my schools, I used to sit next to the nephew of the billionaire, Charles Schwab (why his nephews were in my school, or why I was in theirs, I'll never know). While his nephew was never mean or disrespectful to me, I could not help but notice the glaring contrast between his reality and mine. I often sat there wondering to myself, "why is it that everybody else have new, nice shoes, and new clothes, but my old, oversized, hand-me-down shoes and clothes have holes in them?" "Why does everyone else have a backpack or a lunch pail, but I've never had a backpack, and I don't remember ever having a lunch pail?" "Why is it that everyone seems so happy, but I don't smile anymore?" "Why doesn't anyone want to sit with me?" And, eventually, I began to ask, "is something wrong with me?"

One day, after a very bad night at home, I was sitting in class and my teacher asked the class a question. Like good students are supposed to do, many of my classmates confidently raised their hands to try to answer her question. But not me. I never knew the answer, and sometimes I didn't even understand her questions. However, for some reason, my teacher felt the need to single me out that day and ask me to try answer her question.

I felt my stomach in my throat. "I don't know," I said.

She responded, "but didn't you do your homework last night?"

"I tried, but I didn't understand it," I mumbled. I felt the entire the class look at me in judgment.

She then asked, in a condescending tone, "couldn't anyone at home help you with your homework?"

I tried to explain as best as I could, even though I was terrified of speaking in public. I said, "I asked them for help, but they didn't understand it either."

She then did something that I don't think I'll ever understand. She said, "stand up, please." And I stood up. Then she asked, "why do your clothes look like that?"

In the spotlight of total and complete humiliation, I looked down at my old, oversized, holy, hand-me-down clothes and shoes, then up at her, and said quietly, "I don't know."

"Don't you have a washing machine?" she continued, not noticing that I was on the verge of tears.

"No, ma'am. Well, at the—" I just stopped talking and stared at her, not knowing how to answer that question, and not really understanding why she was asking me those questions. I just stood there staring at her.

She finally ended her inquisition and told me to have a seat.

I sat down, more self-conscious than I had ever felt in my life. I felt dumb, dirty, and stupid.

Later in that same class period, she asked me to come with her into the hallway. I remember walking out of her classroom, into that hallway, nervous and uncertain about what she was going to say or do, for

I was still very embarrassed by the exchange we had just had in class. Once I got outside, she asked me those same questions, again, "why do your clothes smell like that? I can smell your clothes all the way from my desk. You guys don't have a washing machine where you live?" I said, "no ma'am." She then said, "well, I don't want you coming to my class with clothes smelling like that. The other kids are complaining to me that your clothes are stinking up the class."

Then she got closer to me, and looked me straight in the eyes, and said these words, "Young man, if you don't get your act together, and start doing your homework, you are probably going to be like your dad." With kind of a laugh or giggle, she asked, "Isn't he in prison or something?" While what she said was probably true, it did not help me at that moment. It hurt me to the core of my being. She had not learned that timing and tone are important.

I just looked up at that teacher—a woman who was supposed to give me hope, a glimpse of my own possibilities, or clarity about my life's purpose—and just nodded because I saw her and other teachers as extensions of my mother. Since I would never talk back to my mother, I would not dare talk back to a teacher, I reasoned. Nonetheless, that teacher scarred me deeply. Standing there, looking up at her, I was nearly in tears. All I could get out was, "yes ma'am." I went to the bathroom and stayed in the bathroom stall for the rest of the class period to avoid the judgmental faces of my classmates and teacher.

That was just one of many terrible experiences I had at school as a child. From kindergarten all the way through high school, something happened to me that made me dislike school more and more. In kindergarten, I was called a nigger. In first grade, whenever I got a question wrong, my teacher often slapped my desk, scaring me to death. She treated me as though I was stupid, and embarrassed me by constantly raising her voice and yelling at me in front of other students.

In second grade, my teacher often denied my requests to use the restroom even though she let other students use it. As a result, I wet my pants in her class on more than one occasion and had to ride the bus home smelling like urine.

In third grade, although I liked my teacher, Mrs. Elliott, I started falling further and further behind in her class, and started noticing the vast differences between myself and my classmates. It was in third grade that I began to realize that the other kids were smarter than I was, or at least they seemed to be, because they always did their homework and had the right answers in class.

Because I had become aware of how far behind and different I was from my classmates, it was in third grade that I started searching for reasons to not go to school. To avoid school, I often faked sicknesses, I hid my shoes, I "forgot" to set my alarm, and I made up holidays so I would not have to go to school.

In fourth grade, we moved from Aurora, Colorado to Long Beach California, where I was the "new kid" again. Being the new kid was never fun for me. It was scary and lonely. Being the new kid involves walking into a class, having the teacher introduce you to that class, having the class greet you, and you having to say something about yourself to everyone, even if you are terrified of public speaking. In my case, I was timid, shy, and socially awkward. So when I was put in those positions to speak, I started sweating and breathing hard. It was a struggle to just say, "hi."

At lunchtime, I was the kid who sat alone in the cafeteria. I was the kid who got his lunch with lunch tickets, and scanned the room, looking for a friendly or familiar face, only to find none, and ended up sitting at an empty table by himself. The loneliness, the embarrassment, the awkwardness, the self-consciousness of being the new kid traumatized me. I got tired of not fitting in, tired of not being accepted, and tired of not being invited to join people's groups. I got tired of not being asked to birthday parties. I just got tired of being on the outside. So I made the decision to stop going to school.

Instead of going home, and instead of going to school, I spent much more of my time in the streets. It was in the streets that I learned how to survive. It was in the streets that I learned how to steal groceries from supermarkets just so I could have food to help me make it through the night. It was in the streets that I met people who were just as broken as me, just as angry as me, and just as socially awkward as me. They were just trying to find a place to belong, like me. They were not bad people; just broken, lost people. Just like me.

At eleven years old, I was running the streets with some of those guys. It was then that I started smoking marijuana. It was then that I started drinking alcohol. I remember drinking a lot of peppermint schnapps, tequila, Budweiser, Old English 8 ball, Bartles and Jaymes wine coolers, and a bunch of other liquor whose names I do not recall. It was in the streets that I began stealing cars and burglarizing homes and robbing people. It was in the streets that I learned to play cat and mouse games with police officers. It was in the streets when I learned how to find secret getaways, and back streets, and where I learned to identify undercover police officers and unmarked cop cars. It was in the streets that I learned how to survive.

I spent so much time in the streets, wasting so much time, smoking weed, getting drunk, stealing bikes, breaking into houses, and doing a whole lot of dangerous and stupid things that I practically had given up on school altogether. In fact, from fourth grade to ninth grade, I missed 60 to 90 days of school, almost every year. I was out in the streets doing dirt, wasting time, and being idle.

Furthermore, my English grammar was so poor, and the school system was so broken, that I was placed in a classroom with Mexican immigrants who did not speak any English. I sat in that class for nearly one year trying to learn Spanish. That class was designed for native Spanish speakers, and I did not speak Spanish at all! However, because my birth name was Manuel Valentin Sarmiento—a strong Mexican name—someone in my school believed I spoke Spanish. In my memoir, *Turning the Page*, I explain why my mom gave me that name. So I won't get into it here. I will just say that being in that class for native Spanish speakers not only made me hate school even more, but also gave me an empathy for the kind of culture shock immigrants must feel whenever they enter the United States or a foreign country.

I was such a bad student that I earned a 0.6 grade point average the first semester of my freshman year of high school. I earned three Fs two Ds and a C. I received a D in physical education! Nowadays, gym teachers let students wear shorts that go down to their knees. But when I was in middle school, and in high school, we had to wear little shorts that went up to the top of our thighs. They were like little Daisy Duke shorts. They were so short and tight that when you put your little student identification card in your back pocket, people could see your face through the back of your shorts! What I am trying to say is that those shorts were tiny. Also, because I had a tattoo on my left thigh—one that I got when I was eleven years old when I was drunk and high—I could not wear those little tiny shorts to gym class without getting in trouble, or being reported to the office, or, even worse, having my mother find out about my tattoo.

The second semester of my freshman year, my best friend was murdered brutally. When my best friend, Alex, was killed, something inside of me died with him, and I went into a very dark depression. It was in that dark place that I became very angry. I was suicidal. I had gotten to a place emotionally that I really stopped caring about the feelings of other people.

Emotionally, I was dead, spiritually, I was dead—everything about me was numb. I was in such a dark, angry place that I began thinking of ways to force other people feel my pain. It is indeed true that hurt people hurt people because I wanted to hurt people.

It was in that place of brokenness, that place of darkness, that place of death, that I just gave up. I gave up on life, I gave up on hope, I gave up on loving people, I gave up on any dreams, and began thinking things like, "people like me- we ain't supposed to make it!"

It was in that valley of despair, that swamp of misery, that place of utter lostness, that I gave up.

Let me pause right here, and ask you a question: if you saw the younger me that I have been describing standing on a street corner, what could you have done to help me? How could you have tried to reach me? What could you have said? What could you have said to engage someone like the young, angry, broken, lost man I used to be?

If you were walking down the street, and you saw me sitting on a bench, what would you have thought? What could you have done, if anything at all?

How can you try to help someone who looks like he or she needs help? Think about it. Honestly, take some time, and reflect on what you would say, what you could say, or what you should say, to a person is in a bad, depressed situation.

Maybe you have already had some experiences like that. If so, what did you do to try to help someone? Was your approach effective? If you could go back and do it over, would you do anything differently?

Reflect on those questions.

## Two Fundamental Questions

Just before I jump into the meat of this book, I have two questions I would like you to answer. Please turn off any music that's playing, turn off any televisions that are on, and go to a quiet place. Here is the question: DO YOU HAVE A HEAVY BURDEN TO HELP OTHER PEOPLE?

History is filled with people who changed the world because they had a burden to make this world a better place. Although they were not always the smartest, most prosperous, or most influential, they had a heavy burden in their hearts to keep fighting to help others. Their burden gave them the strength and inspiration they needed to keep fighting.

This leads to my second question: DO YOU *REALLY* BELIEVE *YOU* CAN HELP THE PEOPLE WITH WHOM YOU WORK OVERCOME THEIR OBSTACLES TO REACH THIER POTENTIAL? I ask this question because it is fundamental to your effectiveness as a leader. If you have all the degrees and credentials, but do not believe that the people with whom you work are more significant than their circumstances, then you can't really help them. If you know all the "best practices," but do not genuinely believe that the people with whom you work can achieve greatness, then you cannot help them. Instead, by working with them, you will be doing them a great disservice.

If you no longer believe that education can equip your kids to not only realize their potential but also become globally-minded citizens who help make this world a better place for everyone, then you cannot help them. Furthermore, if you no longer believe that the people with whom you work can survive and thrive as productive citizens of the world, then it is unlikely that you will do the things necessary to help them reach their potential.

If you have stopped believing in people, for whatever reason, I pray you do some soul-searching to renew your faith, or that you find something else to do with your life. There is just way too much at stake for you to just be going through the motions, collecting a paycheck, and wasting your life. The most vulnerable people need leaders who are committed to showing up every day to help them flourish as human beings. The most vulnerable people in our world today need teachers, speakers, and leaders who are fully committed to making a difference in their lives.

The best leaders, in my opinion, give a voice and stature to groups of people who have no political power. They don't just speak for marginalized people; they help marginalized people speak for themselves. Our world needs leaders like that.

The best leaders are not—and will probably never be—known on a national level because they are too busy working at a local level to facilitate organized action to improve the conditions of the least, the last, the lost, and the left out. The world needs leaders like that.

The world needs leaders who know how to work within "the system," because they realize that even though the system is flawed, the system can be changed by their presence, their voices, and their influence. We need leaders with burdens like that.

We need leaders who will teach, speak, and lead with a purpose and a passion because they believe that someone's future is tied to their words and actions. Are you one of those leaders?

So I ask again, do you have it in your heart to to be a teacher, speaker, or leader like that? Do you really have a burden in your heart to reach people? Is a burden really there, or is helping others just something you are doing for a paycheck? Is helping others some pet project, or some neat fad that you're getting involved with? Or, is a desire to reach others at the very core of your being?

Do the terrible situations that many people live with bother you? Is someone else's pain something that sometimes keeps you up late at night? Does the pain of other people sometimes cause you to cry a silent tear? Is reaching people something that concerns you so much that, if asked to compromise your convictions, you would rather sacrifice your comfort and even your paycheck before you sell out? That may seem radical to you—and it probably is—but I think that people today are in such a desperate situation, that they are in need of radical people who have a heavy burden to help them.

Because you picked up this book, you may very well be the kind of person who can reach people. Honestly, that is my heartfelt prayer.

CHAPTER **TWO**

# COMMUNICATION 101

Let us begin by laying the foundation for reaching someone. A big part of reaching someone involves communication. Just because we are talking it does not mean that we are communicating. Communication involves so much more than talking. In this chapter, I want to give you a quick overview of my understanding of communication.

First, take about five or ten minutes to try to fill in the blanks that are on the diagram on the next page. It is called Communication 101, and it is tremendously helpful when thinking about the communication process, and working with others. Every word on the left side of the page should fit into a slot on the diagram itself. There are twenty-two words, and each word should fit into one of the twelve spots on the diagram:

- Audience
- Blame
- Desired Action
- Encode
- Environment
- Feedback
- Frame of Reference
- Frustration
- Key to Understanding
- Message
- Nonverbal
- Non-action
- Noise
- Objectives
- Paraverbal
- People
- Resultant Action
- Speaker
- Suspend Judgment
- Technology
- Verbal

Grab a pen and try your best to fill in the diagram.

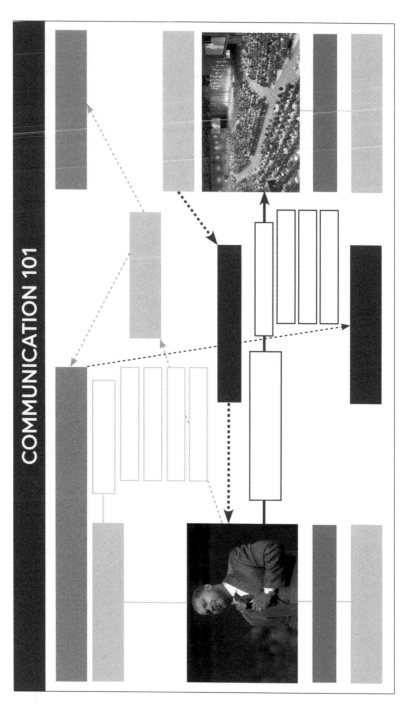

COMMUNICATION 101

Now, let me explain my understanding of how the communication process works most effectively.

At the most basic level, all communication involves a **Speaker**, and **Message**, and an **Audience**. The speaker can be a teacher, a CEO, a parent, student, leader, or anyone who makes a statement. Anytime you open your mouth to speak, you are a Speaker. As a speaker, you have a **Frame of Reference**. Your frame of reference is like a set of glasses that determines what you see, and how you see it. Your frame of reference defines *who* you see, and *how* you see them. It also determines what you want, and how you want it. Your frame of reference shapes the lens through which you see the world. As such, it is out of your frame of reference that you want people to learn something, feel something, and do something. Those things are your **Objectives**.

Out of your frame of reference, you want your audience to learn something, feel something, or do something. What you want people to learn, feel, or do, again, grows out of your frame of reference. However, people cannot read your mind. So you must **encode** your objectives using **verbal**, **paraverbal**, **non-verbal**, and **non-action** to create a message. Then you must open your mouth and deliver that **Message** to your audience.

This is usually where the communication process begins to break down. Why? Because there is often **Noise** between you and your audience. That Noise can be an **Environment** that is too loud or in-appropriate for your message. For example, you could be speaking in cornfield on a windy day. No matter how hard you try, the environment can become too much of a distraction, causing your audience to tune you out.

**Technology** such as cell phones, laptops, bad sound systems, or terrible lighting can also be noise. The more I speak around the country, the more convinced I am becoming that the stronger the internet

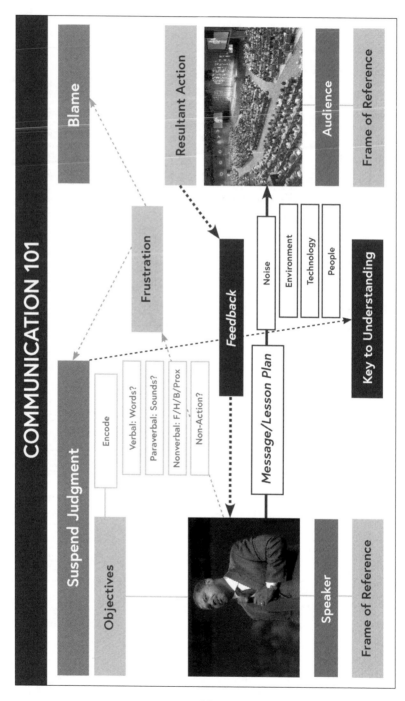

# COMMUNICATION 101

Blame

Resultant Action

Frustration

Feedback

Suspend Judgment

Encode

Verbal: Words?

Paraverbal: Sounds?

Nonverbal: F/H/B/Prox

Non-Action?

Objectives

Message/Lesson Plan

Noise

Environment

Technology

People

Key to Understanding

Audience

Frame of Reference

Speaker

Frame of Reference

connection is, the weaker the human connection. To be sure, I am not against technology; I am just against people not being fully present with the people who are next to them or in their proximity.

Furthermore, **People** can become noise as well. There are few things more frustrating for a speaker than to have loud, distracting people in the audience.

In addition to your challenge of overcoming noise, you must also deal with the fact that, regardless of how clear you believe your message is, ultimately, it is the audience that determines the meaning of your message. That is, *although you as a speaker control your intentions, ultimately, your audience determines meaning*. You can control what you say, but you cannot control how people interpret what you say.

The Message that others hear you delivering is determined by their own **Frames of Reference**. Because people in your Audience probably have an entirely different frame of reference from you, they usually learn something, feel something, or do something—**Resultant Action**—that are entirely different from what you had in mind- your Objectives.

That Resultant Action is **Feedback** to you that the Audience did not really understand your Message in the way you had intended. That realization, that Feedback, often leads to the burn of **Frustration**; and, when we are frustrated, we usually respond in at least one of two ways. First, we can **Blame** or we can **Suspend Judgment**. We can Blame others for not being a good listener, or for not being smart enough, or good enough, or whatever enough. When you Blame others, the problem, in your brain, is them. The problem is the Audience. In your brain, something is wrong with *them*.

Suspending Judgment is another option we can choose whenever we feel frustrated by the Feedback we've received from our audience. When we are frustrated, we can work to avoid forming premature conclusions. We can work to not allow our conclusions be stronger than our evidence. We can withhold our conclusions until we have gathered enough information to make an informed conclusion. Rather than assuming that we have figured someone else out, or that we are sure of their motives, or that we really know what they intended, we can work to suspend our evaluation of them until we gather more information about them or the situation. We can avoid evaluating someone else's character, intentions, intelligence, or behavior prematurely. Why is that important? Because it is entirely possible that the problem is not with the Audience, but with something or someone else. It is also possible that the Message was not Encoded in a way that the audience could understand, or that the Speaker had an ill-conceived Objective.

In any case, I am convinced that it is the Suspension of Judgment that is the **Key to Understanding**. If we want to understand something or someone, it is imperative that we suspend judgment when we feel frustrated.

## Why Frame of Reference is So Significant

I want to show you how this works in real life. When I was in college, I met and fell in love with a beautiful woman named Alice. I was inspired to ask for her hand in marriage. So I flew to Los Angeles, secretly met with her parents, expressed my love for their daughter, and asked for, and received their blessing. Then I proposed to Alice, and she said yes. That was when all fun began. Alice was primarily responsible for planning the wedding, and I was responsible for planning the honeymoon.

I was thinking of taking her to a place with blue waters and white sand, but before I started planning, I wanted to see if there were any places that she dreamed of going for our honeymoon. I'll never forget her response. She said something like, "Well, my sister, and my cousin, and their boyfriends are all going to Italy on a ten-day tour, with a big group … and the trip is going to be right around the same time as our honeymoon. So I was thinking, why don't we spend our honeymoon in Italy with them?" My heart sunk. Not because I did not enjoy the other people who were going to be on the trip, for I really believed I was marrying into one of the most beautiful families in the world. Her family wasn't the cause for my reluctance. I was just concerned that I would have to share my new bride with her family, even though it was supposed to be our honeymoon and not a family reunion.

So I responded with something like, "Babe, you know I love your family. I think they are beautiful and all that. However, the thing is, I was thinking that you and I would go someplace for our honeymoon, alone- just the two of us, together. No one else. You know, the wedding vows said that we are supposed to leave our parents and cleave to one another, so I was thinking you and I could go to some exotic place, and celebrate our marriage. You know? Just us. Just me and you. Just you and I. Just us."

Despite my appeal, we spent our honeymoon in Italy with my new in-laws and a large group of people. On one of the first morning's of the trip, we were all eating breakfast in our hotel's dining room. My wife and I were sitting at a round table with her sister, her cousin, and a couple other people we did not know, but who were in our large travel group. The breakfast was not what I was expecting.

Some danishes were a little different from what I preferred. The orange juice was red, which I had never seen before. There were some eggs, but they were undercooked. I felt something was missing from my breakfast: some bacon or sausage—some hog! Even though I do not generally eat a lot of pork, I just wanted something more for breakfast that morning.

So I said to the group, "Man, I sure would like some bacon or sausage or something." One of the women at our table, who was from another country, but who was also in our group, heard me express my desire for bacon, and reached into her blouse, reached under her breasts, and pulled out a little plastic bag of meat patties! The meat patties were not in a Ziploc bag. They were in one of those little plastic sandwich bags that you flip to close. Well, her bag of meat patties had not been flipped closed. The woman reached into the little plastic bag, pulled out what kind of resembled a meat patty, reached across the table, and offered it to me. She said, in a sweet, generous voice, "Here, please."

I could not believe it! I am not proud of what I did next, but I share it with you because I think you could benefit from my ignorance. Before I knew it, I had a disgusted look on my face, I made some kind of sound that indicated how repulsed I was, and I said, "I just lost my appetite."

Then, to make matters worse, I pushed myself back from the table, stood up, and went back to my hotel room. On my way out of the breakfast room, I looked back at that woman in disbelief and disdain. Again, I am not proud of my behavior, but stick with me because I have a point to all this.

About ten years later, when I was sitting in a doctoral class on intercultural studies with friends who are from around the world, my eyes were opened about what had happened at that breakfast in Italy. My friend from Nigeria explained to me that some women in Nigeria have to walk long distances, and sometimes they carry their children with them. So they bring with them bags, like purses, with food, snacks, and drinks to help them on their journey.

My friend then gently informed me that the woman probably did not pull out the meat patties from under her "business," but instead that she had pulled them out from the purse-like bag that she wore under her clothing. Embarrassed, I began to shrink in my seat. My shame got worse.

Another friend from India said, "Manny, in parts of my country, that woman probably knew who you were, and was probably trying to bestow honor upon you." Another friend from Asia said, "Yeah, Manny, in my country, what you did to that woman is probably one of the most disrespectful things you could have done to us." My friend from Mexico chimed in, saying, "Manny, in my country, when someone wanted something, and we had it to give, my grandmother, and mother, always shared it with them." By the time my classmates were done schooling me, I was so ashamed of myself. I was embarrassed, I was convicted, and I sat there wishing I could go back and have a do-over with that woman in Italy.

Can you see how that relates to my diagram on Communication 101? As a speaker, I have a North American frame of reference. Out of my frame of reference, while I was eating breakfast in Italy, I wanted some bacon or sausage (Objective). I opened my mouth and expressed my desire through a Message. A woman heard me (Audience) through her own frame of reference and pulled out what appeared to be meat patties from under her breasts. That Resultant Action was Feedback to me, and it led immediately to Frustration and Blame. I put my car in park on Blame street. I could not believe that anyone would be so rude as to do something so socially unacceptable and uncouth. I got up with an attitude and walked away. My mind was made up about that woman. I was her prosecutor, jury, judge, and warden.

However, had I suspended judgment that day in Italy, I could have learned something. Had I suspended judgment, I could have asked that woman a question, and perhaps made a friend. I could have learned about her country or some of her customs. I could have learned about her diet or her family. I could have really learned something.

Furthermore, I would have probably grown as a person. However, because I was so committed to blaming her, and committed to pointing out what was wrong with that her, I robbed myself of an opportunity to grow as a person. I delayed my own growth for ten years because my mind was closed about that woman.

You may not be in Italy, but I am pretty sure you have made the same kind of mistakes in your own life. All of us, if we are not careful, can see things through our own frame of reference only, and create unnecessary barriers that divide instead of bridges the could unite us. Generally, when we encounter someone who does something that does not fit neatly into our frame of reference, we conclude that something must be wrong with them. However, we need fewer barriers and more bridges in our world. We need bridges of understanding and bridges of friendship.

Furthermore, when we encounter people and things that do not fit comfortably into our frame of reference, we tend to experience culture shock, which leads to feelings of distress, of helplessness, and of hostility toward new people and new environments. That can present additional challenges for crossing cultural lines.

My hope is that you work to suspend judgement the next time you feel frustrated by people you want to help. You might be justified in your frustration, but you might also be wrong. There is good, bad, and different. In intercultural interactions, give space for people to be different.

## The Basis of the R.E.A.C.H. Approach

The above communication diagram actually lays the foundation for the rest of this book. Often, when I hear people talking about helping others, and reaching others, and empowering others, and so on, but I cringe because very often the person who wants to do the helping is himself or herself in need of help. The helper is usually blind to some of his own assumptions and biases that are being caused by his or her own frame of reference.

So before you talk about reaching others, I think you need to first take a careful look at yourself, and examine your own frame of reference. You carry with you patterns of thinking, feeling, and behaving, and while those patterns may not necessarily be wrong, they might have unintended consequences for you when you try to reach other people.

To be sure, sometimes your background can be very helpful in preparing you to reach a particular group of people. Even then, though, I think it is generally better to examine your own frame of reference because such an examination will help you become even aware of how you might be coming off to other people. Furthermore, such an analysis might help you to understand better how others might be misunderstanding you.

# CHAPTER **THREE**

# FRAME OF REFERENCE

What is the ultimate purpose of life? Of education? Recently, I asked a room full of leaders this same question. Their answers were fascinating. One guy started off by saying that "The ultimate purpose of life is to leave the world better than we found it." Another guy disagreed. He said, "Well, I believe the purpose of life is to experience all of the beautiful landscapes of the world. To travel." Someone else introduced his understanding of education's ultimate purpose, saying, "I believe the purpose of education is to help students realize their fullest potential." Disagreeing, someone else said, "I believe the purpose of education is to help students become world citizens so they can help humanity." We talked for several minutes and their answers were as diverse as a mosaic. How do your answers compare to theirs?

Why do people see things so differently? People often interpret the same things differently because they have different belief systems.

Your belief systems is made up of your views about the ultimate purpose of life; your deepest, core values; your short-term goals; your preferred methods to accomplish your goals and purpose; and, your understanding about how to use those methods and achieve your goals and purpose. All those elements together form your belief system or philosophy of life (see the diagram below). Your worldview, philosophy of life, or your belief system, are what I will loosely refer to as your **Frame of Reference**. So, going forward, I will refer to your belief system, philosophy of life, worldview, and frame of reference interchangeably, for it is through your frame of reference that you interpret the world. It colors and shades the lenses through which you see and experience the world.

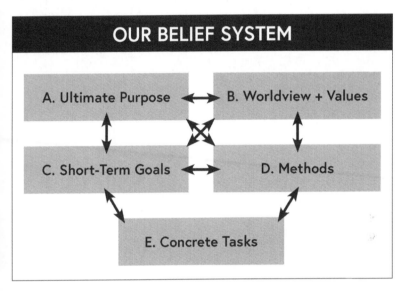

## OUR BELIEF SYSTEM

A. Ultimate Purpose ← → B. Worldview + Values

C. Short-Term Goals ← → D. Methods

E. Concrete Tasks

Your belief system, or your frame of reference, is so influential in shaping your life and choices that we need to spend the next several chapters looking at it more closely.

From where does your frame of reference, belief system, or philosophy of life come? Why do you believe what you believe? Why do you feel the way you feel about things? Why do you do the things the way that you do them? I think the answer can be found by looking at 6 things that shape your frame of reference or belief system.

# HUMAN NATURE

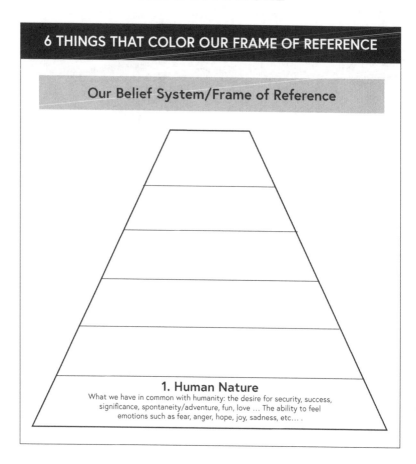

**6 THINGS THAT COLOR OUR FRAME OF REFERENCE**

**Our Belief System/Frame of Reference**

**1. Human Nature**
What we have in common with humanity: the desire for security, success, significance, spontaneity/adventure, fun, love ... The ability to feel emotions such as fear, anger, hope, joy, sadness, etc.... .

First, your frame of reference is shaped by **human nature**. Like other members of humanity, we all have a survival instinct. We have a need to survive. We want to feel safe and secure. We want to be successful and significant. We like to laugh, have fun, and experience love. We all like feel emotions such as fear, anger, love, hope, joy, sadness, and so on. Although we all experience those feelings, how people express those feelings is influenced by their cultures and personalities.

Also, your frame of reference is shaped by heredity, which I will include under human nature because they are so closely related. You inherited certain traits or genes from your parents and ancestors. Your eye color, skin color, and body type were passed down to you from someone in your family tree. We can't really change our genes. We can change how we look by getting plastic surgery or putting on makeup or contact lenses, but we cannot change the genes that were passed down to us.

Your frame of reference is also shaped by your culture. Let's talk about that in the next chapter.

# CHAPTER **FOUR**

# CULTURE

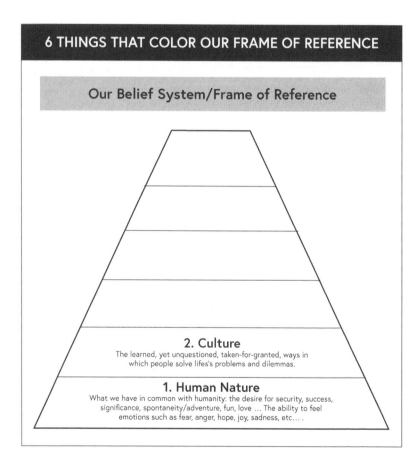

**6 THINGS THAT COLOR OUR FRAME OF REFERENCE**

Our Belief System/Frame of Reference

**2. Culture**
The learned, yet unquestioned, taken-for-granted, ways in which people solve lifes's problems and dilemmas.

**1. Human Nature**
What we have in common with humanity: the desire for security, success, significance, spontaneity/adventure, fun, love ... The ability to feel emotions such as fear, anger, hope, joy, sadness, etc... .

*"Lady, who the hell do you think you are, coming in here with all your white privilege, and your do-gooder attitude? In your brain, you probably see us all as a bunch of*

*savages, animals, chinks, niggers, and spicks! You don't really care about us...You are just like the cops who arrested my father; you had your mind made up about us before you even got here...If you had to choose between a white person or a person of color, you know that you would pick a white person every single time."*

That was essentially how several of my high school classmates felt about our new, young, white student-teacher during her early days with us at Woodrow Wilson High School. Despite all her cheerleader alacrity, which she acquired from growing up in a gated community in Orange County, an affluent area in Southern California; despite her repertoire of "best practices" given to her by her graduate school professors; and, despite her very thorough syllabus, which had printed on it the names of some great European writers such as Chaucer, Hemingway, and Frost, my high school English teacher failed to establish a good rapport with us, her very multi-cultural class.

My high school of 3,500 students was a microcosm of Long Beach, California, one of the world's most ethnically diverse cities. We had over fifty sports teams, hundreds of clubs, and a whole lot of tensions. We were divided by race, class, gender, and interests. With that kind of extraordinary diversity, how can one who works in, or feels called to work in, diverse contexts serve their people more effectively?

Although many educators assume that they are effectively serving their multi-cultural classrooms, I am not so sure. Based on informal interviews I have conducted over the last decade of local, regional, and national school leaders; and, based on the tens of thousands of hours I have spent with diverse groups of young people, I have become increasingly convinced that many of our children might be failing in school and in life because many of their teachers do not understand them. A quick look at the dropout rates of African-American students might confirm this. In 2010, for example, 782,481 of the 2,371,154 African-American students enrolled in high schools dropped out. While researchers have shown that youth delinquency can be attributed to several factors (poverty, systemic and institutional racism, lack of parental involvement, etc.), my own challenging experiences as a child with teachers in many of my public schools has prompted me to wonder how much of the problems facing youth today can be attributed to cultural misunderstandings?

This is significant because your culture as a leader or teacher, if left unexamined, can pose problems for teaching or communicating across cultural lines. That is, when you are socially and culturally different from your students or audiences, you cannot merely assume that your students or audiences share your beliefs and assumptions. That assumption creates distance from your audience and limits their opportunities to learn. Therefore, it is essential that you develop cultural self-awareness.

What exactly is cultural self-awareness? According to the Sage Encyclopedia of Intercultural Competence (2015), "Cultural self-awareness is a person's conscious ability to critically view and understand the objective and subjective cultures to which the individual belongs" (177). On the one hand, "objective culture" refers to the aspects of culture that can be perceived with our senses such as language, music, cuisine, dress, holidays, rituals, and other seeable elements are outward ways in which a group of people expresses themselves (177). On the other hand, "subjective culture" refers to the aspects of culture that are beneath the surface, such as values and assumptions, and cannot be perceived with our senses (178). Intercultural scholars believe that cultural self-awareness is not some innate quality that people automatically possess, but is something that people must learn. They also claim that a person cannot become interculturally competent without first becoming culturally self-aware (178).

This is so important because if you lack cultural self-awareness and cannot ascertain in-depth understandings of your students or audience, then students or audience members who do not share your culture will be disadvantaged academically, socially, or professionally.

I sometimes wonder how many people have been labeled as slow, apathetic, or have been placed in special education courses because of cultural differences. Further still, how many of students have been suspended or expelled from school because their teachers did not take the time or develop the competencies to understand them culturally? What about in the professional world? How many people have been rejected from a job because employers saw their cultural differences as deficient? How many people have been passed over for promotions because supervisors used cultural differences as a reason to conclude that they were not a "good fit?"

This is also important on a practical level because if educators who work in multi-cultural schools lack a basic understanding of their own cultural contexts, teacher effectiveness and morale will decline, teacher turnover will rise, which would exacerbate the quality of education that many kids receive America. Furthermore, there will be an increase in tension between teachers and students (and their families). Those tensions will probably lead to more suspensions and expulsions, which, in the end, will produce an increase in dropouts, teen pregnancies, an ill-equipped workforce, poverty, sickness, violence, and crime. The same can be said about society and companies in general.

These concerns have prompted me to search for ways to equip not only educators but also leaders, speakers, and students with the cultural awareness, knowledge, and skills needed to understand, and more effectively serve, their increasingly multi-cultural students and audiences.

During my quest for answers, I was fortunate enough to enroll in a doctoral-level anthropology course at Trinity International University, where Dr. Robert Priest, one of the nation's most prominent missiologists and anthropologists, led me into a goldmine of cultural anthropology and pointed my eyes toward several gems that are sparkling there. One such gem was Clifford Geertz's (1973) semiotic approach to anthropology. In his book, *The Interpretation of Cultures*, Geertz helped define what anthropology is ultimately about. While reading Geertz, I could not help but think how his approach could help improve the effectiveness of several teachers, leaders, and speakers who work in multi-cultural contexts.

During my presentations to audiences around the country, I often call them to become "students of their students." I encourage them "to study their students like anthropologists study culture." However, I rarely have time to unpack what I mean by that. So, for the next few chapters, I am going to try to explain how you can and should become like an anthropologist in your work, becoming a student of your students.

First, in this chapter, I will define what culture is, and then, in the next chapter, I propose that you subscribe to a symbolic approach to cultural anthropology, which, I believe, can significantly help improve your effectiveness in reaching and teaching people.

## WHAT IS CULTURE?

In *Teaching Cross-Culturally* (2003), Judith and Sherwood Lingenfelter share their knowledge about what teachers can do to become more effective at reaching and teaching people from diverse backgrounds. Their primary claim is that to be an effective teacher, one must become aware of one's own cultural values, and also understand how those values might cause conflict in other cultures. Only after one has become clear about their own biases and expectations can they begin their journey toward effectiveness as a teacher.

If culture is so essential to reaching and teaching others, what exactly is culture? Before I dive deeper into culture, I want to say that culture, ethnicity, and race are not the same things. Although I have heard several people use culture, ethnicity, and race interchangeably, they do not refer to the same things.

Nations or societies have broad patterns of thinking, feeling and behaving. Those patterns are called **culture**. Every nation or society has sub-cultures within them. Some of those sub-cultures are called **ethnic groups**. Ethnic groups are groups of people who collectively identify themselves as a distinct group on the basis of sharing a common language, history, belief system, and common customs. African-Americans, Asian-Americans, and Italian Americans, for example, are are all ethnic groups, or subcultures, that exist within the larger culture of the United States.

So while each ethnic group, or sub-culture, shares some similarities with the larger, macro, culture, it has distinct patterns of thinking, feeling, and behaving. **Ethnicity**, then, refers to an ethnic group's distinct patterns of thinking, feeling, and behaving.

Furthermore, **race**, unlike culture and ethnicity, is a social construct created in the 13th by Europeans to justify the exclusion, oppression, colonization, and the eventual enslavement of other ethnic groups.

I will return to the concepts of race and ethnicity in chapter eleven. For now, I just wanted to help you understand the differences among race, ethnicity, and culture.

Now, I want to focus on culture because it helps me lay the foundation for the rest of the book.

Culture is an agricultural word that comes from the Latin verb, "*colere*," which means "to tend, guard, cultivate, or till." In most Western languages, culture commonly refers to one's cultivation or refinement through formal education. So, in most Western countries, when we say someone is "cultured," we are usually referring to someone who has an informed love for the music, poetry, wine, museums, and literature. This is culture in the most superficial sense of the word.

Culture, in the broader sense, refers to the taken for granted, matter of fact patterns of thinking, feeling, and behaving. Let us unpack that definition a little.

## Culture is Patterned

There are patterns, or rituals, of thinking, feeling, and behaving that get repeated over and over again. How close should we stand to others? What should we eat? What should we not eat? Who should we be friends with? Who is not like us? When we greet each other, should we shake hands, hug, fist bump, nod our heads, say something, kiss, or bow? When we talk to one another, should we maintain eye contact, or avoid it? What about when we are talking to members of the opposite sex? How should we greet them? All these patterns give us glimpses of culture.

Furthermore, those patterns fit into a bigger historical, economic, political, and religious context. We are not a junkyard of history, but really a product of it. So, when it comes to thinking about culture, one question to ask yourself could be, "what is the nature of the order that is here?" Your answer might reveal some of the patterns of your culture.

## Culture is Learned

Our patterns of thinking, feeling, and behaving are not inherited genetically, but they are learned. Human beings are curiously unfinished at birth, and socialization is a part of how we learn culture.

## Culture is Shared

Culture is not only learned, but it is also shared with other people. Culture is learned, but it is learned by virtue of you and I being part of a community that shares that learning. It is a collective phenomenon because it is at least shared with people who live or lived within the same social context. In that sense, culture is a collective programming of the mind which distinguishes the members of one group or category of people from another.

## Culture is Dialectic

Culture is both an objective reality in the world and a subjective reality within people's minds. Berger (1967) says, "society, which is created by human thought and actions, in return, acts upon humans by shaping them. This never-ending process gives humans the power to make, re-shape, and transform culture, even as culture continues shaping them."

## Culture is Multi-layered

Culture exists on global, national, regional, and personal levels. Because of that, elements of culture cross boundaries regularly without compromising the distinctiveness of the different cultures.

## Culture Has Sanctions

Another interesting thing that is important to understand about culture is that you may not always see culture, but you will feel the consequences of it if you break one of its rules. There are informal positive and negative sanctions in every culture, and if you do something that is frowned upon, then you will be punished. If you do something that is desired, then you will be rewarded. Culture, then, being a shared phenomenon, works to bring one into line. It works to make one socially acceptable among a specific group of people.

Let me try to show you how this has worked in your own life. After you were born, when your parents took you home from the hospital, they began, culturally speaking, programming you. By the way they raised you, they modeled for you how you should talk, walk, eat, greet, dress, sleep, live, love and so on. They taught you about who belonged in your group, and who did not. They taught you how people in your group should think, feel, and behave. They taught you how to properly relate to people in your family, in your neighborhood, and in your environment.

Before you were even aware of it, your brain was programmed with those same patterns of thinking, feeling, and behaving. You just took those patterns for granted. Most of us never really question our patterns because we have had them for so long. Those patterns give us glimpses of our culture.

Specifically, what kinds of patterns can you look for when attempting to understand of yourself and of those whom you serve?

## Culture is Functional

Some cultural anthropologists see culture as a body with many different body parts. Just as a body has several different components which serve a specific function of the body, the different parts of culture serve particular functions for a group of people. Scholars have identified several common problems or dilemmas that most groups of people in the world face. Regardless of geography or genetics, nationality, gender, ethnicity, or religion, nearly every group of people encounters some of the following problems and/or dilemmas.

Furthermore, how each group of people responds to those dilemmas/problems is what distinguishes that group as a culture. It is what sets them apart as a group culturally.

Also, their responses to these problems or dilemmas get passed down to their children and shape the frame of reference of every person who grows up in that culture.

Take a look at the diagram below to see my summary of the cultural problems or dilemmas that most groups of people face:

## CULTURE IS FUNCTIONAL

Culture is the unquestioned, taken for granted, patterns of thinking, feeling and behaving which a group of people solves problems and reconciles dilemmas.

There are common problems/dilemmas om tje world that every group of people faces, regardless of geography or genetics: of nationality, gender, ethnicity/race, age, or religion.

| LOW CONTEXT CULTURES | HIGH CONTEXT CULTURES |
|---|---|
| Individualism: I/Me | Collectivism: We/Us |
| Universalism: Right | Particularism: Relationship |
| Low Power Distance: Equal | High Power Distance: Hierarchical |
| Low Tolerance for Ambiguity: Specific | High Tolerance for Ambiguity: Flexible |
| Neutral: Calm | Affective: Demonstrative |
| Achieved Status: Personal | Ascribed Status: Relational |
| Short-term Orientation: Now | Long-term Orientation: Later |
| Active: I can change things! | Passive: I can't change much |

# INDIVIDUALISM vs. COLLECTIVISM

Do you believe your own interests should prevail over your family's interests; or should your family's interests prevail over your own interests? What about your school, or company for which you work? Should your own interests prevail over their interests? Or, should the school's or company's interests trump yours? What about your country? Should your own interests prevail over the interests of your country, or should the country's interests take priority over your own individual freedom? Your answer to these questions reveals the tension that exists between individualism and collectivism.

Collectivism is the belief that the interest of the group prevails over the interest of the individual; and, individualism is the belief that the interests of the individual prevail over the interests of the group. Do you do whatever you want to do regardless of how it will impact your family, classmates, company, or country? Or, do you do what is best for others, regardless of how you feel about it personally?

Both individualism or collectivism have pros and cons. One good thing about individualism is that it helps the individual person reach his or her potential. One challenge of individualism, however, is that it can lead to selfishness and self-centeredness. The USA, Australia, Great Britain, Canada, Netherlands, New Zealand, Italy, Belgium, Sweden, France, Ireland, and several others are predominantly individualistic cultures (Hofstede, p. 53).

The beauty of collectivism is that the group grows and benefits because of an individual's sacrifices. One downside of collectivism is that the individual often disregards his or her own personal interests, and, as such, does not actualize his or her own personal potential. Collectivism is prevalent in Mexico, most countries in Central and South America, countries the Caribbean, Southeast Asia, East Africa, and several other countries.

Where do you fall on that spectrum of individualism and collectivism? Where do your students or audiences fall on that spectrum? Even though some of your students or target audience are in the United States now, did some of them immigrate from other countries? How might that help you understand them a little more?

I'll share how my own personal pertaining to individualism and collectivism. For most of my childhood, my personal community was loosely collectivistic, but was so dysfunctional (my father was incarcerated; my abusive, alcoholic step-father used cocaine; my extended family was not very supportive) that I slowly began subconsciously subscribing to a kind of individualism that involved me focusing solely on my own personal growth and success. Fortunately, individualism helped me personally succeed (13 years of marriage, doting father of three, thriving in many areas of my life, etc.).

Having said that, I have come to see the importance of community. Like the poet, John Donne said, "No man is an island, entire of itself, every man is a piece of the continent, a part of the main." Despite my own individualism, I recognize my need for community. I have not resolved the dilemma, but I am trying to find a healthy balance between focusing on my own growth, as well as seeing about the needs of others in my family, my community, and my country.

I recently read an article questioning why the West is remaining silent about the way people around the world are being persecuted or suffering, and I immediately wondered how much of that silence might be attributed to individualism.

In any case, you need to become aware of where you fall on the spectrum of individualism and collectivism.

# UNIVERSALISM vs. PARTICULARISM

Imagine you are riding in the passenger seat of a car, and a loved one of yours (spouse, parent, sibling, best friend) is driving the car. While riding along, your loved one accidentally runs a red light and slams into a car in the middle of the intersection. The other vehicle spins out of control and drives into a telephone pole, and explodes.

You and your loved one are fine, even though the hood of the car you are in is a little damaged. Your loved one looks around and notices that there are no witnesses around. No one saw what happened. Without saying a word, your loved one speeds off, rushes home, and hides the car in the garage.

Once inside your loved one's home, he or she turns on the television and sees that the crash is on the news. The driver of the car that your loved one hit died at the scene, and the police are looking asking for help. They say on the news, "If anyone has any information about the hit-and-run, please contact us immediately."

Your loved one turns off the television in a panic, and says to you, "I know this is bad, but I just cannot turn myself in. I just can't. I will go to jail for this, and I do not want to go to jail. I'm sorry. Please do not tell anyone about what happened?" What would you do in that situation? Would you try to convince him to turn himself in? If he refuses, what would you do then? Would you keep your knowledge of the accident to yourself, and not contact the police? Or, would you go straight to the police station, and let them know what your friend did? Your response to this dilemma reveals whether you are more of a universalist or a relativist/particularist.

Universalism is the belief that there are universal, objective rules in one's culture which every member of that culture ought to follow. People who subscribe to this kind of universalism tend to value rules or principles over relationships. To be sure, they care about relationships; just not as much as they care about complying to the culture's universal standards. Relativists (or particularists), however, value relationships over rules. They too care about rules, but just not as much as they care about preserving their relationships. This dilemma creates all kinds of conflicts in the world.

For instance, you may have seen this dilemma when it comes to marriage. When someone in your family is planning to marry someone that most people in the family do not like, does the family do anything to stop the wedding, or at least express its disapproval? Many families, despite their criticisms of the marriage, talk privately with one another about their concerns and reservations, but they almost never express their concerns with the family member whom they believe is making the "mistake."

Where do you fall on the spectrum between universalism and relativism? Would you confront the wayward family member because you felt it was your obligation to do so, or would you keep your concerns to yourself for the sake of the relationship?

A universalist, who believes that one should always tell the truth, would perceive the family's reticence as dishonest and unloving. A relativist or particularist would care more about preserving the relationship than they would about telling the truth.

To be sure, particularists believe in telling the truth, but just not as much as they do about protecting their relationships with their loved ones. Saying something, in the relativist's mind, might upset the relative, and possibly harm the relationship.

I am not arguing for you to take any position. I am just trying to get you to get more clear about your own cultural background. This is important because it can help you understand others who might have different cultural convictions about rules and relationships.

# LOW vs. HIGH POWER-DISTANCE

During my first semester at the University of California at Berkeley, on the first day of classes, a professor introduced himself to the class and explained his expectations for the course in a manner that made me very anxious. He told us to call him by his first name, and then said, "A significant portion of your grade depends on your willingness to engage, discuss, and even disagree with me, and each other, publicly, vocally." I sat there quietly, trying to process what was saying. He continued, "I am most impressed by students who will engage in combat with me verbally. I most respect students who argue with me. If you think I am wrong, I want you to say so. Try to change my mind. Persuade me. Push back. Fight for your position." He then confessed, "I must admit that I tend to gravitate toward students who can articulate themselves well, students who are willing to disagree with me. I don't know. There is just something about those kinds of students that I just love!"

While almost all of my classmates were used to that kind of interaction with their teachers, it became painfully clear to me that I was at a disadvantage academically. There was no way I would be able to disagree with him publicly; and, there was no way I would ever call him by his first name. Doing so would have caused me to violate some of my deepest convictions about teacher-student relationships.

Most of my teachers, in high school, college, and graduate school have had a low-power-distance orientation that made school very difficult for me, and, as I look back, that may have been one of the factors that prompted me to drop out of high school.

While some of my difficulty in school may have had a little bit to do with my lack of self-confidence, I am convinced that some of it had to do with power-distance. What exactly is power distance?

Power distance refers to the emotional distance between subordinates and their superiors, or more specifically, to the dependence relationship in a country between those who are in charge and those who are under their leadership. Hofstede (2997, p. 61) defines power distance as is "the extent to which the less powerful members of institutions and organizations within a country expect and accept that power is distributed unequally." In other words, people from high-power-distance cultures subscribe to the belief that inequality exists between leaders and followers. Superiors believe that their subordinates are fundamentally different, and vice versa.

On the one hand, Most countries in Middle (Mexico, Central America, and the Caribbean islands), in South America, in Southeast Asia, India, and several other countries have high-power-distance cultures. On the other hand, most northern European countries, Israel, New Zealand, Costa Rica, USA, Canada, and others countries have low-power-distance cultures (Hofstede, 1997, p. 26).

One's power-distance orientation begins at home. In low power-distance homes, parents teach their children to ask questions, to argue and strive toward independence and self-sufficiency (Hofstede, p. 68). In many North American schools, this low power-distance orientation gets reinforced by curriculum and teachers:

"In the small-power-distance situation, teachers are supposed to treat the students as basic equals and expect to be treated as equals by the students. Younger teachers are more equal and are therefore usually more liked than older ones. The educational process is student-centered, with a premium on student initiative; students are expected to find their own intellectual paths. Students make uninvited interventions in class; they are supposed to ask questions when they do not understand something. They argue with teachers, express disagreement and criticisms in front of the teachers, and show no particular respect to teachers outside of school. When a child misbehaves, parents often side with the child against the teacher..." (Hofstede, p. 69ff).

In low power-distance homes and schools, children are encouraged to argue, express themselves, to "push back," and achieve their own intellectual independence.

Children who grow up in high power-distance homes and schools are culturally very different from ones who grow up in low power-distance ones. In high power-distance homes, children are not encouraged to become independent or self-sufficient. Instead, they are invited to submit to their parents for a lifetime. Their families socialize children to know their place in the hierarchy that exists in the home and in the family. Status is ascribed based on age and other facts.

According to Hofstede, this hierarchy at home is reinforced in school, whereby the student sees the teacher in the same way he or she sees his or her parents:

"In the large power-distance situation, the parent-child inequality is perpetuated by a teacher-student inequality that caters to the need for dependence well established in the student's mind. Teachers are treated with respect or even fear (and older teachers more so than younger ones); students may have to stand when they enter. The educational process is teacher-centered; teachers outline the intellectual paths to be followed. In the classroom, there is supposed to be a strict order, with the teacher initiating all communication. Students in class speak up only when invited to; teachers are never publicly contradicted or criticized and are treated with deference even outside of school. When a child misbehaves, teachers involve the parents and expect them to help set the child straight..." (Hofstede, p. 69)

I share this with you because unlike those who come from low-power-distance homes, students who come from high-power-distance homes experience a severe culture shock when placed in schools that reinforce low-power-distance cultures, and which have teachers with low-power-distance orientations. The people, policies, practices, and purposes in most American schools all work together to create an environment in which low-power-distance norms are often reinforced. Together, these things help to cultivate students who are independent thinkers and self-sufficient. While this is ideal, it can create significant challenges for students who come from high power-distance environments.

But I have gotten a little ahead of myself. For now, I just want you to think about what your power-distance orientation is. Do you come from a high power-distance home, where you were taught that kids are meant to be "seen and not heard?" Or, did you come from a home where you were free to argue, disagree, and participate in adult conversations? In any case, your orientation definitely affects how you relate to others.

High power-distance people tend to see low power-distance people as disrespectful, whereas low power-distance people see high power-distance people as bossy and dictatorial.

Let me tell you about an encounter I had with a young middle-school aged white kid in my neighborhood. Shortly after I moved into the area, I was driving home one day, and I was passing by him. I slowed down, and said, "Hello, sir. How are you?" He responded with a very informal, "wassup?" Even though I usually talk to my friends and my peers that way, I must admit that that young kid's response to me took me by surprise. I couldn't believe that he was so comfortable talking to me, an adult, so informally.

At first, I felt disrespected and wanted to stop the car and give the young man a lesson on how to talk to adults with respect. Then I realized that it is entirely possible that either that young man had not been taught any manners, or that he was being raised in a low power-distance home where he talks like that with his parents and relatives.

The more I have gotten to know that young man, I have come to see that he is actually a very friendly, helpful, smart kid who just happens to live in a home where they have a very low power-distance orientation. This realization has forced me to think twice whenever I encounter someone who comes off to me as disrespectful or too informal.

I share this with you so you can take a closer look at how your own power-distance orientation might affect how you see and interact with others.

## ACHIEVED STATUS vs. ASCRIBED STATUS

How do you determine someone's standing in society? How do you evaluate success? Some cultures accord status based on one's personal achievements. In the United States, for example, we, as a culture, tend to give status to those who have overcome significant obstacles to achieve a goal. We are impressed by people who have started from the bottom and rose to great heights. We like hearing rags-to-riches stories. We are impressed by the grit, the fight, the determination that one has to have to achieve great things. We celebrate people who were once high school dropouts who return to school and graduate from college. We celebrate the person who was once homeless, but, who, through hard work and determination, is now rich. We are inspired by that kind of story, and we accord people status because of it.

However, in some cultures, one's standing in society is not based on personal achievement. Instead, it is based on other factors like age, family, name, profession, education, or some other attribute. In those cultures, it does not really matter that you have gone to college. They are more impressed by *which* college you attended. It doesn't matter who you are. People are more interested in who *your father* is. People are not impressed that you work for a particular company, but they want to know your *position* is in that company. These examples are a bit oversimplified, but I share them with you to help you see that status in some cultures is accorded in very different ways.

If you live in the United States, chances are that you ascribe status based on personal achievement. You are more impressed by what someone has accomplished personally, regardless of who their parents are. While that is not a bad thing, it can become an issue if you are interacting with a family that does not ascribe status in that way. It is essential for you to understand this reality.

# LOW vs. HIGH TOLERANCE FOR AMBIGUITY

Another problem or dilemma faced by every group is their ability to handle ambiguity. Hofstede (1997) refers to the extent to which members of a group or culture feel threatened by ambiguous or unknown situations as "uncertainty avoidance." I refer to it as tolerance for ambiguity. Cultures that have a low tolerance for ambiguity tend to need every little detailed spelled out for them in writing, while people with a high tolerance for ambiguity do not.

According to Hofstede, people in Greece, Potugal, Guatamala, Uruguay, Belgium, Japan, Peru, France, Spain, Turkey, South Korea, in Mexico, Italy, have a low tolerance for ambiguity (113).

People in Singapore, Jamaica, Denmark, Hong Kong, and Great Britain have a high tolerance for ambiguity and probably do not use 100-page contracts for agreements. In some places, your word or a handshake are enough to solidify an agreement between two people. In those cultures, if you lend someone some money, they are much more laid back about when and how they will get it back. If they do look for you to get their money back, that interaction usually does not involve law enforcement, lawyers or judges.

In the United States, we tend to have a tolerance for ambiguity that is neither high nor low. It is right in the middle of the spectrum. While there are some areas of the country where people are more laid back, there are others where people require details spelled out for them to be comfortable. People in places like the Bahamas,, Ghana, and Tanzania,

This reminds me of The Education of Henry Adams, a book written at the turn of the 20th century by Henry Adams, the grandson of US President John Quincy Adams. Written during a time in which many changes were taking place in the world, Adams came to the conclusion that his education had failed to prepare him for the social, technological, political, and other changes that were taking place in the world around him. Even though I read the book once during my college days in the late 1990s, one sentence from the book has remained with me through the years: "Chaos is the law of nature; order is the dream of man." One could argue that the high-uncertainty-avoidance culture in which Adams was raised had failed to help him make sense of all of the ambiguity in the world.

I've also realized that some of my frustrations in my own work have grown out of my own desire to have everything under control. However, there have been times when I have had to reconsider my proclivity for structure and specificity.

For example, once, when I was putting together an agenda with a colleague who came from a culture that had a very high tolerance for ambiguity, I asked him what he wanted to do during a sixty-minute slot of time. With a straight face, he said something like, "I think I'll just go with the flow." I laughed, thinking he was joking. He wasn't. He said, "I'm just gonna go with the flow." I responded, "I can't put that on the agenda. I need something more concrete." He laughed, and said, "No, just put down: 'go with the flow'" Against my low tolerance for ambiguity orientation, I ended up putting those words on the agenda. Then, during the meeting, when we got to the "go with flow" item on the agenda, he flowed very naturally and powerfully. While watching him, I was reminded that there are some things that my own preference for specificity came from my cultural background.

What is your own orientation when it comes to ambiguity? When you plan for a trip, do you need all the details planned out before you leave home, or do you go with the flow? Your cultural background probably has something to do with that.

# EMOTIONALLY RESERVED vs. DEMONSTRATIVE

Another aspect of culture involves emotions. When you talk on the phone, do your hands rest at your sides, or do they move around during your conversation? Do you speak with your hands? When you are listening to music, do you tend to sit still, and just enjoy the music cognitively? Or, when a song comes on, do you start to move with the music? Do you feel an inclination to dance?

Years ago, my wife and I attended a concert at Westminster Abbey in London, England. The boy choir sang some beautiful songs while standing completely still. They did not clap, they did not rock, they did not dance. They just stood there and sang. The audience just sat there too. After each song, the audience politely applauded, and then the room fell silent again. It was beautiful, but it was very different for my wife and me. It was unusual for us, because, culturally, we come from a more emotionally expressive culture than our friends in London. My wife and I were used to choirs clapping, and swaying, and dancing, and moving. We were used to the audience standing on their feet singing along with the choir and participating in the experience. Neither that choir's performance nor our expectations were wrong, they were just different.

This distinction is important because people who come from emotionally reserved cultures tend to see people who are emotionally demonstrative as thoughtless. They sometimes look down upon people who express themselves with emotion. They see passion as a distraction. Conversely, people who come from emotionally affective cultures tend to look at people from reserved cultures as heartless and boring. People from affective cultures have a hard time listening to speakers or singers or performers who are not demonstrative and passionate and emotional in their presentations. If they are not raising their voices, or personally involved in what they are doing, then, from the emotionally demonstrative person, that performer "must not believe" what he or she is saying or performing.

If you attend a black Baptist or Pentecostal church on any given Sunday, you will usually experience a choir singing with its whole being. They are sometimes sweating, swaying, singing, and rocking with all that they are. Some people who come from reserved cultures sometimes see that kind of worship as too emotional and distracting.

If you attend a white Presbyterian church on any given Sunday, you might find the choir sitting in the back of the congregation. My professor told me that his choir sits in the balcony, behind the congregation. When I asked him why, he explained that in their context, the audience would rather listen to the ideas being expressed through song, and listen to the notes being sung or played. To see the choir would only be a distraction. People who come from emotionally affective cultures would probably see that arrangement as unusual and uncomfortable.

I share this with you so that you can determine if you come from a reserved or demonstrative culture. I may return to this later, but

I should say it now. If you are working with emotionally expressive people, then you need to work at being more demonstrative in your interactions with them, because if they can't feel you, it will be hard for them to hear you. Even if you are an introvert, you can still be personally involved in what you are saying or singing. This is just a cultural reality.

# SHORT-TERM vs. LONG-TERM ORIENTATION

There is another problem or dilemmas that cultures face that refers to time. Cultures with long-term orientations foster virtues oriented toward future rewards, while cultures with short-term orientations foster virtues related to the past and present. Some scholars also make a distinction between sequentially-oriented people and synchronically-oriented people. The former have a proclivity only to do one activity at a time, while the latter have the ability to several things at once, like a juggler.

What is your orientation toward time? Are you short-term or long-term orientated? Do you have a tendency to rush things, and need things done right away? Or, do you have long-term goals that you know will require a lot of hard work, patience, sacrifice, and dedication?

The United States is generally very short-term oriented and has a lot of citizens who have a hard time delaying their gratification. If we want something, we want it now. We have fast-food restaurants, with drive-thru windows, because we are always in a hurry. We don't like waiting in lines, we don't like waiting for results. We want everything now.

In some cultures, however, people have a longer view of things. They have very long-term goals and realize that it is going to take a lot of time, maybe even decades, or centuries, to achieve those goals. I am sitting in Paris, France right now as I write this chapter, and cannot help but marvel at the fact that Notre Dame took almost 200 years to build. I will be headed to Milan, Italy in a few days to see its Duomo. That magnificent cathedral took nearly 600 years to make! Even the way they eat dinner in French and Italy is much slower. Generally, the waiters are in no rush to bring out your meals. In the United States, waiters often bring out your entree while you are still eating your appetizer. At a restaurant here in Europe, my wife and I were finished with our appetizer and were just sitting at our table waiting for our entrees to be served. The waiter kindly approached us and asked us if we were ready for our meals. She did not want to rush us. Instead, she was giving us time to enjoy the appetizer and our conversation. During our travels to Europe, we have come to see that many countries here see meals as opportunities for people to converse and connect. If you have a short-term time orientation, you might have a hard time adjusting to those who have a long-term orientation to the world.

## ACTIVE vs. PASSIVE

How does the culture from which you come see the world in which we live? Is there a sense that the world is so complicated, and multifaceted, and intertwined that it is nearly impossible to change anything? Or, were you raised with a feeling that you have the power to change the world? Your response to this reveals your orientation toward nature. Some have an active orientation, and others have a passive one. Those with passive orientations see themselves as small elements in the world, and that their own actions can do very little to change things. Those with an active orientation, however, believe that although they may be small, they have the power within to affect the environment and make changes in the world.

What is your orientation toward the world in which you live? Do you think things are going to stay the same no matter what you do, or do you really believe that you can change some things? In the United States, we tend to have an active orientation when it comes to change. There are several cultures within the United States, however, that have a more passive orientation to the world. Some people have been poor for so long, and have endured so much, and have been beaten down by so many that they do not really believe that they can change anything.

I share this with you because you need not assume that everyone around you believes that they have the power to make a difference in this world. They don't believe that they can change anything, not even their own situations. Before you can help them, you need to understand that it is not a given that people believe they can change their environment or the world around them.

# HIGH-CONTEXT vs. LOW-CONTEXT

I need to say one other thing about understanding how culture shapes your frame of reference. In *Beyond Culture* (1977), Edward T. Hall introduced the terms "high-context culture" and its contrast, "low-context culture." These concepts help us place all of the above variables like power-distance and individualism into two broad categories. High-context culture refers to a culture's tendency to use high-context messages in routine communication. In a higher-context culture, many things are left unsaid, letting the culture itself do the explaining. In such settings, people do a lot more communicating with body language, and facial expressions, and sometimes tones of voice and sounds than they do with actual words. Since a few words can communicate a complex message very effectively to an in-group (but less effectively to outsiders), words and word choice become very important in a high-context environment.

In a low-context culture, the communicator needs to be much more explicit, and the value of a single word is less important. In low-context contexts, then, less is said through cultural symbols, sounds, gestures, and body language, and more is said through the use of actual words.

This choice between speaking styles indicates whether a culture will cater to in-groups, which is a group that has similar experiences and expectations. In the cockfighting story, I will share later in the book, you will see how the Malinese people were very high-context. For now, though, I just wanted to give you some terms to help you describe some things that you have probably encountered, but perhaps didn't know how to describe.

Culture is often functional. A group attempts to solve problems and reconcile dilemmas in its unique context. That is one way to look at culture. This is helpful because whenever you are interacting with someone from a different culture, and you encounter something that does not make sense to you, it would not hurt to run their ideas, feelings, or behaviors through the above grid of variables to see if things become more intelligible to you. I am not saying you need to agree with what you are seeing. Instead, I am proposing that you first seek to understand before you analyze or evaluate; and, I am convinced that the above concepts can help you do that more effectively.

# CHAPTER **FIVE**

# ETHNOGRAPHY

The previous chapter described culture as functional. That is, that culture is a group's response to its environment and dilemmas. This chapter shows that culture is also symbolic. In *The Interpretation of Cultures* (1977), Clifford Geertz, an American anthropologist, comes to our aid when thinking about how to reach people today more effectively. In his essay, "Thick Description: Toward an Interpretive Theory of Culture," Geertz asserts that the concept of culture is symbolic, saying,

"The concept of culture I espouse … is essentially a semiotic one. Believing, with Max Weber, that man is an animal suspended in webs of significance he himself has spun, I take culture to be those webs, and the analysis of it to be therefore not an experimental science in search of law but an interpretive one in search of meaning. It is explication I am after, construing social expressions on their surface enigmatical."

Culture, in his view, is a system of symbols. A symbol is an object, sound, action, or idea to which people arbitrarily assign meaning, and there is no necessary relationship between the symbol and its meaning. The meaning of a symbol is only recognized by those who share the same culture. That is why  Geertz's claims that symbols on their surface are "enigmatical." He argues that all human thinking, feeling, and acting is symbolic:

"Once human behavior is seen as … symbolic action- action which, like phonation in speech, pigment in painting, line in writing, or sonance in music, signifies … The thing to ask is what their import is: what it is … that, in their occurrence and through their agency, is getting said." (p. 10)

By seeing people, and their words, their gestures, articles, and clothes—every aspect of their lives- as symbols that have a deeper meaning, people's lives become like ink on a page, or words in a manuscript, or like an "acted document," which ought to be carefully read, if they are to be understood. He disagrees with those who say that culture is a power that causes people to behave in certain ways and instead argues that culture is better seen as a context that helps us understand peoples' patterns of thinking, feeling, and behaving.

Geertz then extends his metaphor even further. He claims that since people are like manuscripts that should be carefully read, they are also like books which should be "thickly" described. Culture, Geertz says, "is a context, something within which [symbolic discourse] can be intelligibly—that is, thickly—described." Although I do not entirely agree with Geertz that culture is not a power that creates or causes (for culture, through social hierarchies, hegemonic power, and ethnic stratification, does, and has changed language, and inspired resistance), I fully endorse his final conclusion that culture is a context through which all social action can be grasped.

If culture is symbolic, or an "acted document" that must be read, or a "context" that makes social action intelligible, then it is imperative for you to find ways to read those texts (or construct a reading of them). That is the primary task of anthropology, and anyone using the tools of anthropologists. As such, ethnography the subject to which we now turn.

## "THICK DESCRIPTION"

One of the key terms in Geertz's symbolic framework is "Thick Description." According to Geertz, the primary task of anthropologists is to do ethnography, which is "thick description." He says,

"Ethnography is thick description. What the ethnographer is doing is in fact faced with ... is a multiplicity of complex conceptual structures, many of them superimposed upon or knotted into one another, which are at once strange, irregular, and inexplicit, and which he must contrive somehow first to grasp and then to render .... Doing ethnography is like trying to read (in the sense of 'construct a reading of') a manuscript—foreign, faded, full of ellipses, incoherencies, suspicious emendations, and tendentious commentaries, but written not in conventionalized graphs of sound but in transient examples of shaped behavior." (p. 10)

Anthropologists do ethnography, and ethnography is "thick description." In other words, Geertz believes that anthropology's primary task is to explain cultures through thick description, which should entail not only describing a behavior, but also its context, in such a way that the behavior becomes meaningful, or intelligible, to an outsider. Why is that important?

The significance of thick description is that it supplies a means by which you can "expose a culture's normalcy without reducing its particularity (p. 14). The knowledge we gain from thick description allows people access to "another country heard from" (p. 23). One of the primary purposes of creating thick descriptions is to help people see how others see the world.

"Thick Description" specifies many details, conceptual structures, and meanings to give someone who is not a part of that culture a framework through which to make sense of what is going on. It should contain not only facts but also commentary, interpretation, and interpretations of those comments and interpretations. The ethnographer's, or educator's task, is to extract meaning-structures that make up a culture because a factual account alone is insufficient. The meaning-structures within a cultural context are layered complexly—one meaning-structure is so intricately intertwined with another meaning-structure that each fact or "symbol" might be subjected to intercrossing interpretations.

It is these meaning-structures that anthropologists should study, for without a knowledgeable understanding of those meaning-structures, the ethnographer is left with nothing more than a "thin description," which is a factual explanation of some behavior without an interpretation of that behavior to help people understand its deeper meaning. Put simply, "thick description is the rendering (explaining to others through writing) what the symbols of a culture mean from the point of view of the people who are a part of that culture.

One of the implications of producing a "thick description" of a culture is that an anthropologist must first try to grasp (see/understand) a culture's structures of meaning before he or she tries to render it. Furthermore, to grasp, one of the elementary prerequisites of anthropology is to do one's best to interpret things from the actor's point-of-view (as opposed to the participant-observers'). However, to grasp an insider's understanding of a symbol or culture, an anthropologist ought to strive to converse- speak to or with- the people of a culture, before he or she tries to speak for them. Geertz agrees, saying,

> "We are not, or at least I am not, seeking either to become natives (a compromised word in any case) or to mimic [a groups culture]. Only romantics or spies would seem to find a point in that. We are seeking, in the widened sense of the term in which it encompasses very much more than talk, to converse with them, a matter a great deal more difficult, and not only with strangers, than is commonly recognized." (p. 34)

To learn about the structures of meaning within a culture, the ethnographer must learn to speak the host culture's language. It is doubtful whether one can be bicultural without also being bilingual.

Words are vehicles of culture transfer. Without knowing the language, one will miss a lot of the subtleties of a culture and be forced to remain an obvious outsider.

To grasp a cultural context, one must not only learn to speak to the people that culture, but ethnographers should also aim to study in places, not about them. Geertz confirms this, asserting, "The locus of [an ethnographer's] study is not the object of study. Anthropologists don't study villages (tribes, towns, neighborhoods...); they study in villages" (p. 22). This has tremendous importance for you. I will discuss those things momentarily.

By doing these things, and thinking about them in the above manner, an anthropologist (and educator) can increase his or her chances of obtaining a "thick description" understanding of a culture. Even though an ethnographer's knowledge will grow in "spurts" (p. 25), and he will never get "to the bottom of things" because cultural analysis is intrinsically incomplete (p. 29), anthropologists must still work toward gaining a first-person, actor-oriented perspective of symbolic action. Geertz reassures, that while one's interpretations may not be completely accurate, "it is not necessary to know everything to understand something." (P. 20) When constructing a reading of a person or culture, the ethnographer is doing his or her best to understand something of the webs of significance that a group of individuals has themselves constructed.

In his essay titled, "Deep Play: Notes on the Balinese cockfight," Geertz provides an example of what thick description looks like. Read this carefully, because it gives you a sense of how you too can work in your own context to gain a thick-description understanding of the people you want to reach. Geertz describes the ritual of cockfighting that he and his wife observed as anthropologists in Bali in 1958. Upon their arrival, the people of Bali ignored them. Despite their best efforts to establish some kind of rapport, which he refers to as the "mysterious necessity of anthropological fieldwork" (p. 416), the people of Bali ignored them. In the eyes of the Balinese, they had not yet achieved the status of "existence." Though the Balinese were aware of what Geertz and his wife were up to, they chose not to acknowledge, or even interact meaningfully, with the outsiders (p. 413). These informal negative sanctions indicated a form of rejection, or perhaps neutrality, toward outsiders.

Ten days into their visit, they attended a cockfight. Cockfighting, except for a few events, was illegal in Bali at the time. His first observation of the cockfight was raided by the police. Instead of identifying themselves to the police as guests, and distancing themselves from the people participating in the cockfight, Geertz and his wife ran away from the police like the Balinese villagers. The Balinese locals interpreted the running of Geertz and his wife as a demonstration of solidarity, as an affirmation of the Balinese way of life. That gesture (running) transformed Geertz and his wife from invisible, "gusts-of-wind" (p. 413) into the accepted "co-villagers" (p. 416). "[Running from the police] led to a sudden and unusually complete acceptance into a society extremely difficult for outsiders to penetrate" (p. 416). That acceptance was marked by the villagers teasing Geertz and his wife (p. 416).

With this newfound acceptance into society, Geertz began an exploration of the cockfights in detail. In doing so, he discovered that cockfighting was such an intense portrait of Bali life that Balinese compared heaven to the mood of a man whose cock has just won, and hell as the metaphysical and social suicide of the loser (p. 421). Not all cockfighting was considered this important, however. Instead, Geertz suggested that there were times—what he called "deep play"—when both parties in the cockfight entered a relationship likely to bring net pain (p. 433). Geertz found it interesting that, although some might argue this deep play is unethical, Bali men passionately and repeatedly partook in these activities. As such, cockfighting—and the betters who participated—formed a "socio-moral hierarchy" (p. 435). The cock-fight is a symbolic revelation of what Balinese "are really like." As much of America surfaces in a ball park, on a golf links, at a race track, or around a poker table, much of Bali surfaces in a cock ring. For it is only apparently cocks that are fighting there. Actually, it is men." (p. 417).

Through a very microscopic analysis of Balinese webs of significance, Geertz asserts that the cockfight is a ritual through which Balinese men and their social groups channel their rivalries, and compete for prestige and status. He argues that although gambling occupies a central role in the Balinese cockfight, there is a lot more at stake in the cockfight than economic reward. When it comes to the cockfight, prestige and status are much more important than money. To illustrate his point, Geertz describes the distinction between "deep fights," which involve high wagers, and "shallow fights," which involve low wagers. A "deep fight" is a fight in which the stakes of status and prestige are so high that people lose their rationality. The cockfight is a fight for status, and the wagers being placed merely function to symbolize that risk is involved. Although participants in the "deep fights" are usually influential members of a society, the cockfights are not between individuals, but rather between social groups. The cockfight is a simulation of social structure as well. People do not make wagers against a cock that represents their own groups. The cockfights always involve a battle between people from opposing social groups. In that way, the cockfight is the most pronounced expression of a rivalry between two social groups, and it is a meaningful, symbolic way through which the Balinese people ventilate such rivalries.

Whether a cockfight ends in victory or defeat, the status that a Balinese gains or loses as a result of the fight is only temporary. One's overall status in the group is not permanently damaged. Like the status of an American football fan who may get teased because his team has lost a big game, Balinese men essentially maintain their overall status in their communities. With every cockfight, there is an opportunity to regain or reassert, one's supremacy. So just as a North American football game is just a football game, a cockfight, in the grand scheme of things, is just a cockfight.

The "deep play" of the Balinese cockfight, says Geertz, is like a piece of art which illustrates an essential insight into our very existence. The art is a symbolic manifestation of something we perceive to be very real in our social lives. It is a channel through which we ventilate our emotions and understandings of ourselves and the world around us. Thought about in that way, then, the cockfight symbolizes, and participates in shaping, the social and cultural structures of the Balinese people.

Geertz concludes that rituals such as the Balinese cockfight are like a text which can be read and understood, even if the text consists of a chicken hacking another mindlessly to bits (p. 449). He says, "[t]he culture of people is really an ensemble of texts, texts which are themselves ensembles which the anthropologist strains to read over the shoulders of those to whom they properly belong (p. 452), and recommends that on whatever level anthropologists decide to read these texts, societies and lives contain interpretations to which one must learn how to get access.

## IMPLICATIONS FOR REACHING PEOPLE

Geertz's manner of analyzing a culture is advantageous because it sheds light on how you might consider entering, reading, and describing the culture of the people you want to reach. I have identified at least four implications that, if embraced by leaders who work in multi-cultural settings like my high school, could aid them in their quest to engage, reach, and teach more people.

## See People as Actors

One implication of Geertz's approach is that you should see people as actors of (cultural) scripts. Over the last fifteen years, I have asked school administrators about the biggest challenges they face in their schools, and I have lost count of how many times someone has said their teachers were their problem, namely, how their teachers held unhealthy views of their students. I think Geertz's metaphor, of seeing students as actors of a script could serve as a healthy corrective for teachers who have a tendency to label their kids inappropriately. For example, if teachers began to see that every one of their students (and everyone else with whom they come into contact) is acting out a script of learned, shared, integrated, patterns of thinking, feeling, and behaving, they would probably approach their students, and their jobs, a little differently.

Perhaps they would be more hesitant to dismiss, ignore, or punish some students. Understanding that what teachers were seeing was merely a reflection of an unseen web of significance, teachers could begin to see that perhaps their first job as a teacher is to become a student of their students. Teachers would see their need to learn more about the contexts in which their students were raised. If teachers would humble themselves in that manner, I believe they would begin learning things about, from, and with their students.

## Search Symbols for Meaning

A second implication flows from the first; namely, those who work with people should constantly be studying symbols and their meanings. Most anthropologists I have read agree that cultures continuously adapt to the changing world around them. As a result, the meanings that cultures give to symbols is also dynamic. To learn about the interpretations of these symbols, teachers would do well to frequently ask, "what does that mean?", "What is the nature of the order that is here?" What are some patterns?"

Teachers and leaders should be asking their students questions about the meaning of their symbols, heroes, and rituals. What music do they listen to, and why? Who do they admire, and why? What are they wearing, and why? Why are some students wearing Cortez Nikes (attire for the East Side Longos, a Latino Gang in Southern California)? What might that mean? Why are some students wearing grey (attire of the Tiny Raskal Gang, a Cambodian gang), and what does that mean? Why are some students sagging their pants, and what does that mean? Why are so many African-American young men wearing extra-large white T-shirts? What does that mean? What tattoos do they have on their bodies? What do those tattoos mean? What might they be trying to communicate through such art? Of all the tattoos they could have gotten, why did they choose that one? Geertz has helped me see that these kinds of questions can help teachers begin to understand the students who show up in their classrooms every day.

Indeed, such questions can help teachers understand how their students see themselves, others, and the world around them. The more questions a teacher asks, and the more answers they receive, the higher their chances of learning and understanding their students.

I think this manner of asking questions is also helpful because, long before I had heard about semiotics or Geertz, I learned that some symbols had potentially deadly consequences. For example, in my neighborhood, the color red was tied to the Bloods, a street gang that began in Los Angeles and is now all over the country. The color blue was worn by their rivals, the Crips. If one wore a red hat, or red jersey, and walked, or drove a red car, in an area where some Crips resided, then a Crip in that neighborhood would have probably interpreted those things as a threat, or as an intentional encroachment upon their territory. Either of those things would have been seen as the ultimate sign, or symbol, of disrespect. Even though one's love for red might have had nothing to do with gang membership, by wearing red, that person could have unknowingly put himself at risk being of confronted, assaulted, or even killed.

For someone who did not grow up in neighborhoods like mine, they might deem that unfathomable. However, Geertz's' semiotic approach gives you a way to make such behaviors more clear and intelligible. That kind of understanding is something that is greatly needed in public schools today.

## Acknowledge Interpretations are Proximal

This leads to a third, related, implication. You need to acknowledge that your interpretations of others are, in fact, interpretations. For you to effectively teach, speak, or lead in multicultural contexts, you need to understand how your own assumptions, interpretations, and evaluations of others have been shaped by your own cultural background. I believe that this kind of self-awareness could also help you identify any bias or prejudice you might have about people.

Duane Elmer, a former professor at Trinity International University once described this kind of ethnocentricity much more eloquently during one of his lectures, affirming,

"There is a fine line we unconsciously cross that causes the majority of [intercultural] problems. When we think we are normal, we make the rather fatal slip into believing that we are also the norm by which everything and everyone else can be judged. We do this without thinking. But every time we make a negative attribution we risk saying rather loudly to those around us, 'That's not like me. Therefore it is inferior, wrong and unacceptable.'"

Leaders need to work to make sure their interpretations are as close to the interpretations of their students as possible so they can help reduce the potential for cultural misunderstanding, or worse, cultural chaos. This leads to the final implication I would like to discuss.

## Speak *To* Before Speaking *For* or *About*

My high school English teacher once said that she was trained to teach by professors who had not seen a kid in over one-hundred years. She had professors teaching her about students even though they had not recently spent any time with students. As a result, my teacher had to learn about teaching in our multi-cultural school the hard way- trial by fire. Realizing that none of the methods she had been trained to use on us were working, she humbled herself and spent time trying to get to know us. Although she began as an outsider, her humility, and her loving manner demonstrated to us that she valued us, and respected our cultures. As a result, we let her in and accepted her.

She visited our homes and got to know our families. She asked us to give her tours of our neighborhoods, and even invited us to introduce her to some of the neighborhood drug dealers! She listened to us as we discussed our heroes, our music, and our cultures. Because of her commitment to enter our world, the magic of learning began to take place in our classroom. I believe that if you adopted that kind of approach—spending time with your students or audience in their contexts, and talking to them—you would become much more informed and qualified to speak for and about people. This is not insignificant.

When you earn the trust of people in that way, people will begin to share relevant, sometimes confidential information with you. Teachers and speakers who spend quality time with the people they want to help, in their contexts, have a much higher chance of learning about things that could have transformational significance.

As a result of reading this chapter, I hope you adopt an anthropological approach to culture, really becoming a student of your students (or adults), and effectively studying them like anthropologists study culture. By doing so, I believe you will begin to identify patterns of thinking, feeling, and behaving that give you clues to your groups unique webs of significance.

## CHAPTER **SIX**

# FIVE CIRCLES

In the last several chapters we talked about your frame of reference, and especially about how your culture affects how you see the world. But how precisely do you identify whether someone is an individualist or collectivist? How can you tell whether they have a low tolerance for ambiguity, or whether they are active or passive? How can you get at someone's belief system or their core values? I have found the below diagram with concentric circles to be helpful.

In the diagram, there are five concentric circles. The outer three layers give us a glimpse into the inner two layers. Because you cannot see someone's beliefs or values by just looking at them, all you can do is look at their symbols, heroes, and rituals.

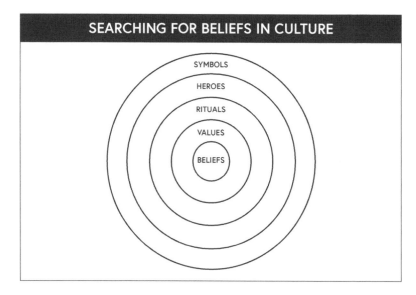

**SEARCHING FOR BELIEFS IN CULTURE**

SYMBOLS
HEROES
RITUALS
VALUES
BELIEFS

# SYMBOLS

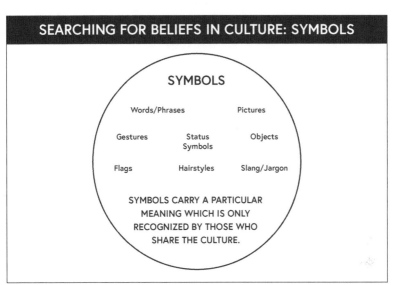

Let us start with symbols. Symbols are words, sounds, gestures, or objects that mean something that is only recognized by those who share the culture. The words in a language, including slang or jargon, would fit into this group. Jewelry like wedding rings and necklaces are symbols. Tattoos are also symbols. Clothing and hairstyles also fit here. What people drink, and the colors they wear, or the bandanas they have on, or the flags they fly are all symbols. The kind of cars that they drive, or the kind of homes they live in, are symbols of something much deeper.

In some neighborhoods, the color red is tied to the bloods, and the color blue is linked to their rivals, the crips. If you go into certain neighborhoods wearing the wrong colors, you could very well become a target. If you wear a red hat, or red jersey, or are driving a red car in an area where crips reside, then they could interpret your presence as a threat, and as a sign of disrespect. They could see you as intentionally encroaching upon their territory. Even though you might just like red, and are not affiliated with any gangs, that does not necessarily change how you will be seen in certain neighborhoods.

Symbols within cultures are fluid. New symbols are easily created, and established ones fade away. Another fascinating thing about symbols is that symbols from one cultural group are often copied by others. Because they are so easy to adapt and copy, symbols are the most superficial way of identifying someone's deeper values and beliefs. That is why symbols are on the outer layer of the diagram.

The main thing you want to ask yourself when you see symbols is, "what might this symbol mean to this person?" Let us use a tattoo as an example. When you look at someone with a tattoo, chances are they were trying to express something about their deeper values and beliefs. Even if you don't understand what the tattoo means, ask yourself, "what might this person be trying to communicate to the world about his or her deepest values and beliefs?"

## HEROES

Heroes are the next layer of culture that we can observe to determine someone's deeper values and beliefs. Heroes are people, living or deceased, actual or fictitious, who have attributes and characteristics that are highly valued in a culture, and who serve as role models for behavior. Even cartoon characters and people from fantasy books and movies can be heroes. Batman, or Harry Potter, or Heath Ledger, or Tupac Shakur, or Beyonce, or Slipknot, or Vicente Fernandez, or Pele, the soccer player might all be heroes to someone. The question you need to ask yourself is what is it about this "hero" that this person values or venerates? Why is this person a hero?

## SEARCHING FOR BELIEFS IN CULTURE: HEROES

### HEROES

HEROES ARE PERSONS,
ALIVE OR DEAD, REAL OR
IMAGINARY, WHO POSSESS
CHARACTERISTICS THAT ARE
HIGHLY PRIZED IN A CULTURE,
AND WHO SERVE AS MODELS
FOR BEHAVIOR.

Not too long ago, a teacher who grew up in the suburbs of a lovely homogenous town, and who is a new teacher in a diverse, poor, inner-city school, told me that one of her students said to her that his mother, who was in jail, is his hero. Perplexed by his answer, the teacher asked me, "Why would anyone consider his imprisoned mother a hero? That seems stupid." She laughed in disbelief.

While I understood her question, I also understood how that student saw his mother as a hero. Despite her being locked up, that mother could still very well be that boy's hero for any number of reasons. Maybe, I suggested, his mother was defending herself against a violent boyfriend, but could not prove that it was self-defense. Perhaps his mother had been through so much in life, but instead of giving up, she has fought to keep her family together. Maybe she is a hero in her son's eyes because she is the most reliable person he has ever met. Or perhaps she is his hero because she has overcome some of life's most difficult circumstances, and is still alive. Who knows? Maybe she is his hero because she went to jail defending her son.

If she had dug deeper, that teacher might very well have discovered very little in that boy's mother that was worthy of reverence. On the other hand, she might have learned something about that mother that was quite honorable and inspiring. Without digging deeper, there was no way of knowing why that boy said his mother was his hero.

As a young man, some of my teachers thought my heroes were stupid too. Growing up, I loved Tupac Shakur because he gave a voice to my anger and frustration as a young man growing up in the inner city. I also looked up to Snoop Doggy Dogg because he had a swagger that I wanted. He was just so smooth. Some of my teachers disdained Tupac and Snoop. They never asked me or my friends why we loved their music.

Also, I used to have posters of Jerry Rice on my wall because I wanted to be a great football player. I also used to watch the movie, Rambo, over and over again because I loved how he was a loner who could survive even in the most life-threatening circumstances. My heroes expressed my most profound struggles or aspirations.

Who are some of your heroes, and why? What is it about them that inspires you? Your heroes are a clue to some of your deepest values, beliefs, and assumptions.

Who are the heroes of the people you want to reach? Who do they look up to? Who do they admire? Who do they emulate? Why?

## RITUALS

Rituals also give you a clue about your deepest values and beliefs. Rituals are collective activities in achieving a specific goal. The rituals themselves do not necessarily mean anything, but which, within a cul-

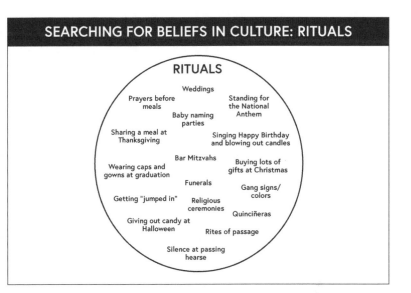

**SEARCHING FOR BELIEFS IN CULTURE: RITUALS**

RITUALS

Weddings
Prayers before meals
Standing for the National Anthem
Baby naming parties
Sharing a meal at Thanksgiving
Singing Happy Birthday and blowing out candles
Bar Mitzvahs
Wearing caps and gowns at graduation
Buying lots of gifts at Christmas
Funerals
Getting "jumped in"
Gang signs/colors
Religious ceremonies
Quinciñeras
Giving out candy at Halloween
Rites of passage
Silence at passing hearse

ture, are considered socially essential. Rituals are thus carried out for their own sake. The way we pray or don't pray, before meals. The way we stand for the National Anthem. The way Americans share a meal at Thanksgiving. These are all rituals. Others include baby naming parties, weddings, funerals, giving out candy on Halloween, singing happy birthday and blowing out candles are all rituals. Buying lots of gifts at Christmas or some other holiday.

When I was younger, whenever a funeral procession was driving by with a hearse leading the way, my family and I always stopped, removed our hates, and "paid our respects." When someone died, even if it was a stranger, there was a reverence that we were taught to have at passing hearses. That ritual reflected a much deeper value and belief about life and death.

What are some of your rituals? What do those rituals mean? Why do you do them? What do they reveal about your deepest values and beliefs?

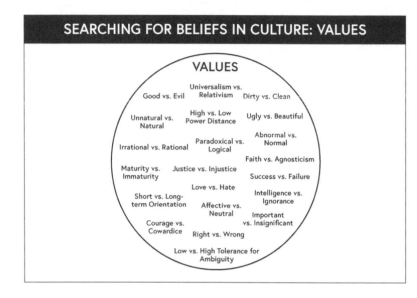

## VALUES

Now we move on to the next concentric circle of values. What are values? Values are broad tendencies to prefer certain states of affairs over others. Values are feelings that have a plus or minus side attached to them. They deal with: evil versus good, dirty versus clean, ugly versus beautiful, unnatural verses natural, abnormal versus normal, paradoxical versus logical, irrational versus rational, and so on.

What is important to note about values is that each of them has different meanings depending on whom you ask. What is evil to you might be considered good to someone else. What is dirty to you might be clean to someone else.

For example, when I was growing up, what was deemed to be dangerous to most people was considered fun to my friends and me. Running from the police was fun to me. Smoking weed was cool to me.

Because values mean different things to different people, you need to understand what you mean when you refer to a particular value. What does it really mean to be "good?" The more you analyze core values and assumptions you hold dear, the more clearly you will understand what you mean when you think about them, or talk about them with others.

My professor told a story of how he and his colleagues flew to Africa to teach English to some young adults. When it was time to take a test, they had to administer several tests to accommodate the large number of students who wanted to take the test. The students who took the first test failed miserably, but the students who took all the remaining tests got all the answers right.

How did that happen? Well, the teachers suspected that the students from the first test went out and started telling all the other would-be test takers what was on the test. To teach the students about the importance of not cheating, the teachers called a meeting. The head teacher asked a question to the student body, "What is cheating?" One of the students stood up and said, "Cheating is having what my brother needs and not sharing it with him." That, my friend, is precisely what I'm talking about when I talk about values. What was cheating to the American teachers was not considered cheating to the African students. In your own journey, you need to get clear about what you mean when you refer to values.

Another example is related to modesty. In America, showing one's breasts would is not generally considered appropriate, or "modest," but in the French Riviera, seeing topless women at beaches is common. Furthermore, in the United States, people are generally expected to be clothed, but in some cultures, body painting is considered appropriate attire. Further still, in Western societies, the more breast a woman shows, the more sexually she is perceived by others. However, in some African cultures, showing legs, not breasts, is considered sexual. Modesty, and every other value, means different things to different people.

What are some of your deepest values? When you say something is "beautiful" what do you mean? What makes it beautiful? Try to get specific. What about "maturity?" What does it mean to say someone is mature? Or dirty? Or bad? What is love? Why do you define it that way? Your answers to those questions reveal some of your deepest assumptions and beliefs that undergird them.

## BELIEFS

Finally, your beliefs, and their underlying assumptions, are at the core of your philosophy of life, your worldview, or frame of reference.

What is the purpose of life? Is the purpose of life to acquire individual wealth or fame? Is it to promote the reputation of the extended family? Is it to please God? Is it to be happy? Is it to live a sacrificial life for others? What about the nature of reality? Is there a God, and if so, does God know me and care about me? Is there an afterlife? Does the physical world really exist, and if so, is it orderly? Are people good or bad? Do people have free will, or is life controlled by the environment? Do evil spirits and angels exist? Is there such a thing as absolute truth? These philosophical and theological presuppositions influence the way you think, feel, and act. People are aware of some aspects of their worldview or belief systems, but most of them are not aware of the assumptions beneath those beliefs.

Going forward, I would like you to pay closer attention to the symbols, heroes, and rituals in your life. When you notice something, try to understand what each one might reveal about your core values, beliefs, and assumptions. Also, try to look for the symbols, heroes, and rituals in the lives of those you would like to help. Ask yourself, "how might these things function in this person's culture? What might this symbolize for this person or group?" I can't stress enough the impor-

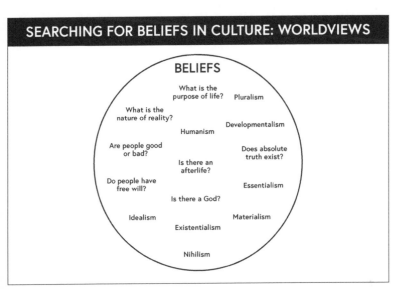

tance of trying to understand people and things before you analyze or evaluate them.

I have spent all this time talking about culture because I think it is imperative for you to understand that almost all your expectations are culturally-based. I also want you to see how your own cultural background has influenced you.

We live in a multicultural world, and I want you to do well in it. I am convinced that if you are going to reach and teach people today in our increasingly multicultural world, you must first seek to examine your own cultural values. That is, you should aim to develop cultural self-awareness. While interacting with others, and trying to understand them, you should also reflect on how similar to, or distant from, them that you are culturally. Understanding your own culture and your own assumptions and expectations about how people "should" think and act is the basis for your success in reaching and teaching and leading others today.

# CHAPTER **SEVEN**

# EXPERIENCES

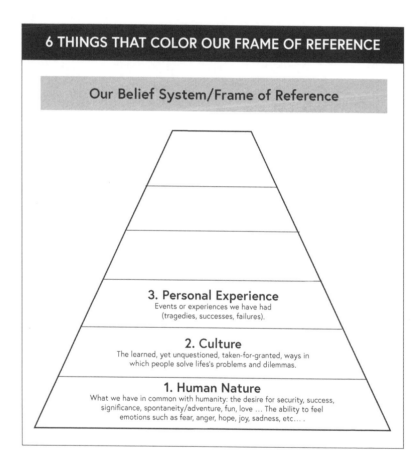

**6 THINGS THAT COLOR OUR FRAME OF REFERENCE**

Our Belief System/Frame of Reference

**3. Personal Experience**
Events or experiences we have had
(tragedies, successes, failures).

**2. Culture**
The learned, yet unquestioned, taken-for-granted, ways in
which people solve lifes's problems and dilemmas.

**1. Human Nature**
What we have in common with humanity: the desire for security, success,
significance, spontaneity/adventure, fun, love ... The ability to feel
emotions such as fear, anger, hope, joy, sadness, etc... .

Have you had any personal experiences that deeply affected your development as a person? What did it teach you, about yourself, others, about life? Have you taken a vacation or a trip that changed how you saw the world? Have you had any jobs that shaped your own personal ambitions?

I'll never forget one of my first jobs at a well known fast food restaurant where I made $4 an hour. I was a junior in high school, and I used to go to that job every day after school. I used to make the sandwiches, mop the floors, wash the dishes, clean the fry machine, and spend a considerable amount of time in the freezers checking on our products.

After about three months on that job, I became really motivated to do something else with my life. I realized then while cleaning out those dreaded fry machines that fast food work was not for me. I needed to go to college and do something that would allow me to make a living and a difference with my mind. I do not knock anyone who is working at a fast food restaurant making an honest living. I just learned that working there was not for me. Because I realized that that kind of work was not for me, I started working even harder at school. Have you had any jobs like that?

Did you grow up in a home with two parents? One parent? How did that shape your values and beliefs? While reflecting on my 12-year wedding anniversary, I realized that I don't have a reference point of what a healthy, happy marriage looks like. Other than what I have seen on The Cosby Show, I have not had a real-life example of how to build a healthy, happy marriage. I have never been close enough to a man who has been happily married. Sure, I've known a few men in my life who have been married, but I have not spent enough time with any of them to know what their marriages were really like. I never observed how they handled disagreements or how they resolved conflict? I did not get to see how they navigated discussions about money, faith, children, in-laws, disappointment, fear, or success?

Even if their marriages were solid, I did not have the privilege of spending enough time with them to observe how they dealt with challenges that I have faced as a man, husband, father, and friend.

The fact is, my father never married my mother, and was not around for most of my life. My first step-father and mother separated when I was five years old. My second step-father was married to my mom for under a decade.

To be sure, I once had a pastor who seemed like he had a good marriage, I was barely fifteen years old, and I could not have cared less about the subject of marriage.

Given that reality, I have asked myself, "Despite my lack of exposure to how marriages really work, how have my wife and I been able to have such a happy, healthy, and fulfilling marriage? Why are things working out so well? Shouldn't I have ruined it by now?" I will be the first to say that a lot of it has to do with the great woman I married. My wife grew up in a very healthy home, and was raised by parents who have been married over 60 years. So, by observing the healthy patterns of her parents, she learned a lot about how to make marriage work. While that may be true, my wife could not have made our marriage work by herself. I had something to do with the success of our marriage as well. What did I do and why did I do it?

As I reflect on the road I've taken, it has become clear to me that a lot of who I am today as a man and husband, and how I live my life, is partly because of what I have been running from. For years, I have been driven by the desire to be different from the men who hurt my mother during my childhood. I've been running from the examples of those men. I never wanted to be like them. Some of them partied and went to nightclubs all the time, so I decided that I would not go to parties or nightclubs. Some were alcoholics, so I decided that I would not drink alcohol. Some were drug addicts, so I decided that I would not do drugs (although I did go through a phase of getting drunk and smoking weed before I made the decision to turn my life around).

Some men were verbally and mentally abusive, so I made a decision to never call women out of their names. Some were physically abusive, so I made the decision never to put my hands on a woman. Some cheated, so I made a decision that I would never violate my wife's trust. Most of them spent very little time with their children, so I made a decision to one day love, cherish, play with, and cultivate my children. I have been running pretty hard to be a contrarian.

Upon further reflection about how I have been able to enjoy such a rich and fulfilling marriage, it has become more apparent to me that it might also have something to do with what I have been running to. I have been running to a very particular future. For me, when I think about the final moments of my life, I have a picture in my head of what I hope those moments will be like. I hope to have my wife there. I see myself holding her hand, and looking into her eyes, one last time. I see us reminiscing about our life together. I see us smiling, one more time, at all of the great, and fun, and silly things we did to bring ourselves and others joy (like we did on our honeymoon in New Orleans, when we danced in the hotel elevator thinking no one could see us, only to be greeted, on our way out of the hotel, by security and staff whose huge grins hinted that they had been watching our elevator routines on hidden cameras. We were so embarrassed! But we kept on dancing, even harder, giving them some of the most ridiculous dance routines that they would never forget).

I share that with you to help you see how personal experiences have a way of shaping your frame of reference. Do you have any powerful experiences that had such a significant impact on how you look at the world? I am sure you have. Your experiences do not have to be negative.

Maybe you have had a powerful religious experience, and it shaped the way you see people and things. Perhaps you are a more loving and forgiving person because of a personal experience you had at a worship service, temple, mosque, shrine, or festival.

My best friend's death made me appreciate life so much more. Being homeless made me much more sensitive to the needs of homeless people. Seeing my mother get abused made me decide that I would never put my hands on a woman. Seeing how drugs and alcohol really harmed many people in my family, I decided that drugs and alcohol would not be a part of my life. Those experiences really shaped me.

Maybe you didn't go through the things I went through, but perhaps you have experienced some things that had such a profound impact on you that they altered the course of your life. Whatever those things are, they have shaped your frame of reference.

In the same way, those things have shaped the frame of reference of the people you would like to reach. It would not hurt for you to try to learn about some of the experiences of the people you serve. I can't tell you how many times teachers have told me that their lives were changed when they opened themselves up to learn about the lives of their students. Personal experiences have a way of shaping how you see the world.

# CHAPTER **EIGHT**

# **PERSONALITY**

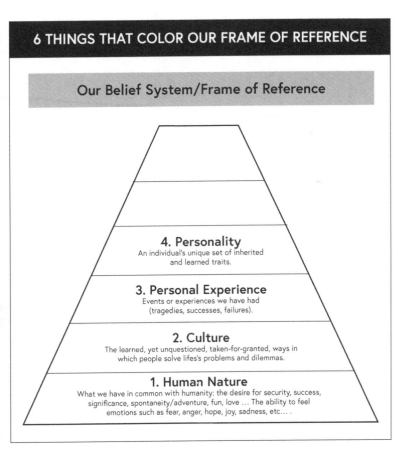

**6 THINGS THAT COLOR OUR FRAME OF REFERENCE**

Our Belief System/Frame of Reference

**4. Personality**
An individual's unique set of inherited and learned traits.

**3. Personal Experience**
Events or experiences we have had
(tragedies, successes, failures).

**2. Culture**
The learned, yet unquestioned, taken-for-granted, ways in
which people solve lifes's problems and dilemmas.

**1. Human Nature**
What we have in common with humanity: the desire for security, success,
significance, spontaneity/adventure, fun, love ... The ability to feel
emotions such as fear, anger, hope, joy, sadness, etc... .

In addition to being shaped by human nature, heredity, culture, and personal experiences, you have also been shaped by your personality. Even though you share the same nature as other humans, and you share the same culture with others, your personality sets you apart from others. Your personality, though influenced by human nature, and influenced by your cultural background, and influenced by your personal experiences, is something that is unique to you.

You might be an introvert who feels drained when you're around crowds; or, you might be an extrovert who gets energized when you are around other people. You might have a dominant personality that drives you to get things done. Or you might have an influential personality, which enables you to work well with other people. You might have a more precise personality, which compels you to be very meticulous with minute details. You might have a very supportive personality, which leads you to prefer to work behind the scenes. No matter what your personality is, it is unique to you, and it has a great deal to do with who you are and where you are in life.

The creators of the DISC analysis have argued that there are essentially four types of personalities in the world. There is the person with the Dominant personality who tends to be direct and decisive. They tend to have high self-confidence and are risk takers and problem solvers, which enables others to look to them for decisions and direction. They tend to be self-starters. Their downside is they can be argumentative and not listen to the reasoning of others. They tend to dislike repetition and routine and may ignore the details and minutia of a situation, even if it's important. They may attempt too much at one time, hoping to see quick results. Do you have a dominant personality? Dominant personalities can sometimes be abrasive and come off as harsh to people who do not understand them. I know this because I have a dominant personality.

Then there is the Influencer. Influencers are enthusiastic, optimistic, talkative, persuasive, impulsive and emotional. They genuinely enjoy being around others, and function best when around people and working in teams. They tend to be great encourages and motivators of others, and they keep environments positive. Though not wholly accurate, influencers tend to be more concerned with people and popularity than with tangible results and organization. Are you an influencer?

Or maybe you have a Supporter personality. People with supportive personalities are steady, stable, and predictable. They are even-tempered, friendly, sympathetic with others, and very generous with loved ones. They tend to be conscientious and are good at multi-tasking and seeing tasks through until completion

Their challenge is that they are generally opposed to change and may also hold grudges when they experience frustrations and resentments.

Or, maybe you are an Anchor, someone who is accurate, precise, detail-oriented, and conscientious. They think very analytically and systematically and make decisions carefully with plenty of research and information to back it up. When something is proposed, it is the anchor who will think through every detail of how it works and the process. Anchors tend to avoid conflict rather than argue, and it is difficult to get them to verbalize their feelings. They can be bound by procedures and methods, and find it difficult to stray from order. Finally, they can get too bogged down in the small details, making it difficult to see the next steps or big picture.

If you had to pick two of the above personality types, which would you choose to describe yourself best? What would your closest friends and colleagues say about you? Would they say you have a dominant personality or more of a meticulous one? It is essential to understand your own personality because it is very possible that others misunderstand you because of it.

Because I have a dominant personality, I realize that I need to soften things when I am talking to people who are influences, supporters, or anchors. I know that I need to give more details when I am talking to anchors and that I need to be less structured when talking to influencers. This kind of knowledge about myself has helped me maintain decent relationships with most people.

How might others be misunderstanding you because of your personality type? In any case, I share this with you so you can be aware of how your own personality type might be perceived by others with whom you work or serve.

What personality-types do the people you want to help have? Try to describe their personality types. What about your co-workers? Your supervisor? Your spouse?

# CHAPTER **NINE**

# EDUCATION

## 6 THINGS THAT COLOR OUR FRAME OF REFERENCE

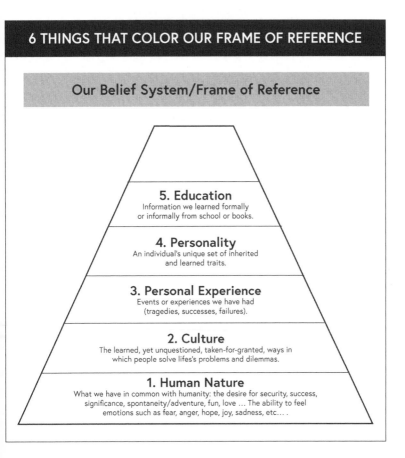

### Our Belief System/Frame of Reference

**5. Education**
Information we learned formally
or informally from school or books.

**4. Personality**
An individual's unique set of inherited
and learned traits.

**3. Personal Experience**
Events or experiences we have had
(tragedies, successes, failures).

**2. Culture**
The learned, yet unquestioned, taken-for-granted, ways in
which people solve lifes's problems and dilemmas.

**1. Human Nature**
What we have in common with humanity: the desire for security, success,
significance, spontaneity/adventure, fun, love ... The ability to feel
emotions such as fear, anger, hope, joy, sadness, etc... .

Your frame of reference has also been shaped by your education. There
are two kinds of education, the kind that others give to you, and the
kind that you give yourself.

# Education That Others Give You

The first kind of education is the one you receive at school. The second kind is the one you get by reading books and other learning opportunities that were not assigned to you at school.

You are shaped by both kinds. I talk to many young people who say they "hate" school. They feel as though school is not related to their everyday lives. I understand how they feel, because the truth of the matter is, I used to hate school, too. I hated reading, I hated writing, and I hated math. I hated being called on in class by my teachers because I hated being embarrassed every time I gave the wrong answer. After letting people know that I hated school, I let them know that I had to change the way I viewed school. I had to change the way I viewed books. I had to change the way I viewed math. Ultimately, I had to change the way I viewed myself.

Changing my perception was so important because I thought I wasn't as smart as the other students. They always seemed to have the right answers. They had better clothes than me, they had better things than me, and it even seemed like the teachers liked them more than me (I know for a fact some teachers did like other students more than they liked me).

Even though those things were true, I had to ask myself, "If I don't take school seriously, how am I going to end up?" It didn't take me long to realize that I would end up like many people in my family who didn't take school seriously. They were working jobs that they hated, they were living in poor neighborhoods, they were living in tiny apartments, they were always fighting over money, and they always seemed miserable. Many of them were in prison, some were alcoholics, and some were addicted to drugs. I know that none of them planned on ending up that way. I also know that society makes it harder on some people than on others.

However, I also made up my mind that I refused to be poor. I refused to be on drugs. I refused to be an alcoholic. I refused to live in poor neighborhoods unwillingly, and I refused to be just like some of the people that I had grown up around—people who drank, smoked, wasted time and money.

I decided that even though it would be hard, I was going to take school seriously. I began seeing books as conversations waiting to be picked up. I started to see math as a game or a puzzle that needed to be figured out. I began to view homework as an opportunity to get better as a person. I started to see school as a way out of poverty, depression, and despair.

Once I made that decision, I started treating my teachers better and began developing better relationships with the adults around me. I knew that not all of them really cared about me or my success, but I also know that there were several who genuinely cared about me, and who wanted me to be my best. I developed relationships with those teachers, and to this day, I thank them for pouring much of their lives into me.

That is the kind of education that others give to you. It's the kind that leads to diplomas, degrees, and certificates.

## Education You Give Yourself

The second kind of education is the kind that you give to yourself. You may not get a degree for this kind of education, but it certainly makes a bigger impression on you. To give yourself an education means that you don't have a teacher, instructor, professor, parent, or some authority figure holding you accountable for the books you read, and the papers you write. You don't have any quizzes, tests, midterms, or final exams to take. This is the kind of education that requires you to buy books on topics that you are interested in. It is the kind of education that causes you to stay up through the night because you are so enthralled by the things you are learning. It is the kind of education that nobody can take away from you.

When I was in college, most of the things I learned were learned from books that were not assigned to me by my professors. I used to complete my assignments for class, and then go to the library and stay there for hours, reading books about rhetoric, argument, philosophy, English, Spanish, geography, politics, law, and society. I became a student whose thirst for wisdom and knowledge was so insatiable that I would often stay at the library until two or three in the morning, even when school was out of session. I often went to bookstores, and just looked through every section, trying to find something that could help me become a better, more knowledgeable person. To this day, I love books, and I have thousands of them that continue to inspire me, sharpen me, and equip me to make a difference in the world.

In the same way, your education has shaped your frame of reference. It has affected how you see the world. Take a moment to reflect on any teachers you have had who have changed your mind or life. Think about books you have read or lectures you have read that had a profound impact on you. Think about speakers you have heard at professional development seminars. All of those things have shaped your frame of reference as well.

Also, think about the education of the people you serve. What kind of schools did they attend? Urban? Suburban? Rural? Title 1? What kinds of classes and teachers have they had? How might those things have shaped or shaded that person's frame of reference?

Furthermore, Sharan B Merriam, in *Non-Western Perspectives on Learning and Knowing* (2007), asks several questions that can help you think about your own culturally-conditioned cognitive categories. They also help you think about the cognitive categories of your students (p. viii-ix). In your culture:

- What is the purpose of learning or going to school?

- What is the nature of knowledge? Is it passed down from one generation to the next or is it constructed? Is there a body of knowledge to be learned? If so, where is this body of knowledge? In people' memories? Embedded in everyday life? In stories and myths? In books? Oral or written or both?

- How is this knowledge learned? Through practice, memorization, apprenticeship, formal classes?

- How is it known when one has learned? Who decides that one has learned?

- What is the role of the teacher? Who can be a teacher?

- What is the end result of learning? A better, more moral person? A wise person? an independent/interdependent person? A knowledgable person? A better community? A more equitable society?

- What is the role of society, community, and/or family in learning?

- How does this perspective on learning manifest itself in your students' lives today?

Now, after you have answered those questions for yourself, you need to ask them about your students or audiences. Then you need to compare and contrast your perspectives.

# CHAPTER **TEN**

# IMAGINATION

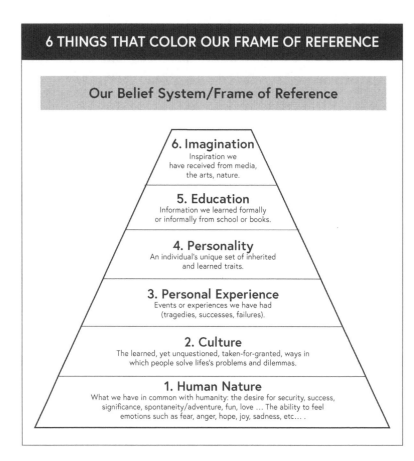

**6 THINGS THAT COLOR OUR FRAME OF REFERENCE**

Our Belief System/Frame of Reference

**6. Imagination**
Inspiration we
have received from media,
the arts, nature.

**5. Education**
Information we learned formally
or informally from school or books.

**4. Personality**
An individual's unique set of inherited
and learned traits.

**3. Personal Experience**
Events or experiences we have had
(tragedies, successes, failures).

**2. Culture**
The learned, yet unquestioned, taken-for-granted, ways in
which people solve lifes's problems and dilemmas.

**1. Human Nature**
What we have in common with humanity: the desire for security, success,
significance, spontaneity/adventure, fun, love ... The ability to feel
emotions such as fear, anger, hope, joy, sadness, etc... .

When I was still a young man in high school when I was still learning the basics of English grammar—long before I became a public speaker—a substitute teacher in my history class put on a video of

Martin Luther King's "I Have a Dream" speech. I had never been more inspired in my life. Watching that man speak from the depths of his soul inspired by something that was beyond this world impacted me in powerful ways. While listening to him and watching him speak, I got goosebumps, and something in my heart said, "you are supposed to do something like that with your life." From that moment, I have never been the same.

From that moment, I began seeing visions of myself standing before large groups of people, inspiring them with words that I was speaking. Sometimes, when I heard other speakers make presentations during assemblies, I often saw myself delivering my own message in their place.

The same thing happened to me in college, at the University of California at Berkeley. Because of these visions of myself speaking to large crowds, I often mentally transformed my little bedroom into a coliseum where an old upright speaker became my podium, and all the objects in my room became my audience. For hours I would recite poetry and speeches in my empty room.

During college, I worked for pennies as a Loss Prevention Specialist—a fancy name for security guard. It was my job to secure the buildings by making sure all the doors were locked, the lights were off, and the place was empty. Many nights, after all the buildings were secure, I went to the largest ballroom in the building (Pauley Ballroom), and for hours, I recited speeches to an empty room.

Eventually, I found myself doing that in the largest venues on campus (such as Wheeler Auditorium), which sat over seven hundred people. I even found a way to practice a few times on the platform of the eighty-five-hundred-seat Hearst Greek Theater. Even though each venue was empty, in my mind, I was speaking to a standing-room-only crowd of people who were being inspired by my words. I would speak as though the room were packed to capacity with people who needed to hear what I had to say. I would speak, inspiring thousands, painting for them a vision of a brighter tomorrow. I would speak, telling people that in spite of where they come from, they can achieve their dreams. I would speak, and I would see, in my head, lives being changed.

Mentally, emotionally, and behaviorally I was committed to making that dream a reality, and it all started with my imagination being inspired. Because I saw a man speaking on a video, I was inspired to start reading books about speaking, and studying some of the world's most influential speakers. When I went to sleep, I had dreams about speaking, and, in my dreams, I saw lives being changed. I saw people being moved by my words. You could not tell me that those dreams were not real, because everything about them affected my body physically.

Sometimes I would wake up from those dreams, and I would be sweating. Sometimes my heart would be racing. In those dreams, I had conversations with my role models. In my dreams, I remember walking around with the Rev. Dr. Martin Luther King Jr. I used to watch him, and listen to him, and learn from him- in my dreams!

I also saw Frederick Douglass, and others, close up, in my dreams. I saw myself speaking before audiences, in my dreams. As I write these words, my heart is beginning to speed up, because I remember those dreams so vividly.

Around that time, people began to invite me to be the master of ceremonies for campus events. I became the guy who was on the microphone engaging, entertaining and empowering audiences, young and old.

Shortly after that, I began receiving invitations to speak to elementary and middle school students. Then I began receiving invitations to speak to high school students. Before long, I began receiving invitations to speak to community organizations. Eventually, I began receiving invitations to speak in other states. Finally, I began to receive invitations to speak in other countries.

I share these stories with you to help you see the power of the imagination. Our imaginations have the power to shape our frame of reference so much that they control what we see and how we see it.

Do you have any inspirational encounters that have shaped your life? Any dreams, stories, movies, songs, performances, paintings, or landscapes from nature? Think about it, because imagination, too, shapes and colors your frame of reference.

What about the imaginations of your students or audiences? What movies, books, stories, or songs have shaped their imaginations about the world? Reflect on those things.

In the next chapter, I need to address the concept of race because it plays such a big role in how we see the world. Because of its pervasive influence on us, it deserves its own chapter.

# CHAPTER **ELEVEN**

# **RACE**

After I spoke to a group of high school students in a small, homogenous town whose citizens were predominantly of European-descent, a young woman sent me a message that described her prejudices against me before hearing me speak. She said, "I was sitting in a classroom a few days ago waiting to fall asleep as some black guy—a stranger—was preparing to talk to a group of [white] high school students. I was thinking ahead to what your sob story would be, what a waste time your speech would be, how you would not be able to relate to us on "our level," and how soon it would hopefully be over with." She eventually went on to apologize for her wrong "assumptions" about me and thanked me for giving her a new perspective about "black people," for giving her hope, and inspiration to improve her own life.

That was not the first time I have heard such sentiments being expressed. In fact, that young woman's ideas are probably more common than one would like to believe. But how did she get those ideas about black people? What would lead her to think that the color of my skin would determine the content of my speech, my intellectual capacity, and my qualifications as a speaker?

More specifically, I wondered, how did people of African descent, or "black people," come to be seen as ignorant, lazy, governed by caprice, intellectually inferior, and devoid of civility? I started doing some research and learned some things that I hope can help you become a better servant-leader in this multi-cultural world.

The idea that one's biology and behavior is predetermined by one's skin color has a fascinating and complex history. Before I get into the origin and history of race, I want to make sure that you understand that race and ethnicity are not synonymous. They are not the same thing. Ethnicity, on the one hand, refers to the set of cultural ideas held by an ethnic group that has a shared history, language, customs, and traditional beliefs. Ethnicity has existed for thousands of years. Race, on the other hand, is a social construct that was made up much later.

## The Origin and History of "Race"

In his book, *Race: The History of an Idea in the West*, Ivan Hannaford meticulously argues that race as an organizing idea- a lens through which much of the world is seen today- was remarkably absent in the ancient world.

He says the seed of the idea of race did not emerge until the 13th to 16th centuries. However, it was not until the 17th century that the idea of race was legitimized by the scientific community. For example, European scientists, basing their research on Darwin's theory of evolution, developed the theory of Unilinear Cultural Evolution, which is the theory that all cultures evolve from simple to complex along a single trajectory of progress. They argued that societies that had social and political systems such as market economies or democracies had "higher development" while cultures that did not have market economies or democracies had "lower development." Not surprisingly, the northern European scientists who developed that theory defined northern Europeans as having progressed to having the "most Culture," while non-European people were seen as less evolved, living in a simpler, less civilized, less "cultured" state. For decades European and U.S. Anthropologists use Culture to classify societies as higher or lower on a scale of cultural development. This lead people to believe that one person could have more "Culture" than someone else.

That unexamined ethnocentricity through which European and American scientists saw ethnic "others" skewed their analysis and their conclusions, thus reinforcing the ideological racism that had been laid in previous centuries.

With the scientific authority behind them, Europeans saw race as a means by which to justify the exclusion, oppression, colonization, and the eventual enslavement of ethnic others. In fact, scholars have pointed out that the very idea of race emerged as an informal ideology that legitimated slavery and oppression of African and indigenous people.

It was in Jamestown, Massachusetts, that we catch a glimpse of the nascent stages of race in the United States. When the British began to settle in the New World and sought to make a profit, they initially hired indentured servants from Europe to work the land. However, because those indentured Europeans knew the language and looked like their overseers, they could escape and blend in with people who had settled in other colonies, the British quickly realized that they needed another plan.

At that point, the British turned to Native Americans, forcing them into indentured servitude. However, because Native Americans knew the terrain better than their European masters, they, like their European predecessors, escaped and returned to their families.

With no labor force in place, and with the trans-Atlantic slave trade becoming increasingly efficient, the British decided to purchase African slaves. Because African captives did not know English, the language of the settlers, they did not share the same British culture, and because they did not look anything like the British settlers, African slaves had a much harder time trying to escape. After all, they could not blend in with other settlers. Therefore, Africans were deemed the perfect solution to the British problem regarding labor.

The British became so dependent on those African slaves that they created categories to make their arrangements permanent. In his book, *In the Matter of Color: Race and The American Legal Process: The Colonial Period* (1978), Higginbotham explains that "This preference for African labor was institutionalized in custom and law. Within thirty years of Jamestown's founding, color terms began to appear in colony legislation. For example, 'negro' servants could be held for life, but not 'whites.' The idea of race, or color, then, was created to subjugate African slaves and make sure that their enslavement ended in death only.

With these arrangements in place, race became a marker, a banner, for social status. What those in power did not realize is that the meanings they attributed to race were a mirror of the political and social realities that they had created. Of course, because Africans and people of African descent were denied the opportunities to get educations and develop culturally, it would make sense that they could not read, write, or excel in other, more culturally refined, areas. Their realities were the consequence of the social and political conditions under which they lived, not their biological make-ups. Blind to their own ethnocentricity, the British equated "black" as someone who was inferior, undeserving of rights, and incapable of being civilized. Black symbolized savagery, ignorance, lacking intelligence, and uncivilized.

Although almost no scientist or anthropologist today would argue that race, as we have described it, exists ontologically (in real life), the consequences of such an ideology pervade the world today and have shaped what we see and how we see it. The fact that a young girl of European descent would question my legitimacy as a speaker, and question my intellectual capacity because of my skin color is a remnant of centuries of systemic racism. That system must be dismantled, and

I believe that parents and educators are in the best position to help eliminate the power that "race" has in our world.

I once took a course that was taught be a well-meaning, genuinely nice, white psychology professor who said that black people need "a new narrative," and that we need to stop bringing up slavery. She argued that slavery is in the past, and we need to "move on." We asked her if she would say the same thing to Jewish people who lost their family members in the Jewish Holocaust. To her credit, she was consistent. She said that Jewish people need to move on too.

We calmly and lovingly tried to explain to her how we, her African-American students, have living relatives who were born so close to the end of slavery they still have the stench of slavery on them. We explained that some of our relatives have seen family members lynched by white mobs during Jim Crow; and, we tried to help her see that their stories and struggles and pain live on through us, their descendants. We also tried to explain that the system that oppressed our parents and ancestors has not been completely eradicated.

Exasperated and frustrated, she asked, "What more do you guys want?" It became clear that she had not been taught how crippling slavery and Jim Crow has been on the development of black people in America and around the world.

That conversation helped me see that there are many good, sincere, educated people- of all ethnicities—who have never really learned about the race, ethnicity, and slavery. So if you would allow me the opportunity, I want to describe an experience with you that I hope gives you a more accurate picture of slavery. I share this because I am not sure it is being taught to students in many public schools. However, because this topic is so important, I hope it helps to enlighten someone.

## A First-Hand Look at the Cape Coast Castle

I recently took my family to Ghana so we could visit the Cape Coast Castle and learn about our family history. Most of the enslaved Africans who were shipped to the United States, the Caribbean, and the Bahamas began their journeys from the Cape Coast Castle. So it is very likely that my wife's and my ancestors passed through the castle.

Cape Coast Castle, Ghana

During our visit, we stopped by Palaver Hall, which was derived from the Portuguese word that means "bargaining." Palavar Hall was the "auction block" of the Cape Coast Castle where slaves were divided by sex and age before being sent to the dungeons for up to three months.

Palaver Hall

Trade between Europeans and Africans was based on a barter system where goods were exchanged for slaves, who weren't considered human beings, but property. African slaves were exchanged for dyed cloths, iron bars, brass, and shells. For example, in 1714, an African woman from the Gold Coast was traded for the equivalent of 7 guns, 22 sheets, and 2 small cloths. In 1731, the English could buy 40 slaves with 40 muskets, 337 trading guns and 530 pounds of gunpowder. Five male slaves could be traded for 30 guns, 40 pounds of gunpowder, and 39 sheets. At one point, a slave could be exchanged for 100 gallons of rum, 100 pounds of gunpowder, which had a cash value of $20" (Nguah and Kugbey, 2015, p. 51).

On the auction block, "captives were kept in groups like animals and auctioned one by one. The buyers, before they purchase, examined their ears, eyes, teeth and whole body for deformities to determine their health status. Subsequently, they were branded and given new names. The re-naming practice broke their spirit and separated families forever as parents and children could be bought by different masters." (Nguah and Kugbey, 2015, p. 51)

## Male Slave Dungeons

We also spent some time in the Male Slave Dungeons.

The dungeons held up to 1,000 male slaves at a time. The men and boys were fed just enough to keep them alive, and were forced to urinate and defecate on the floors. There was so much feces on the floor that it piled up to about 1 or 2 feet along the wall. You can still see how high the excrement was by the marks along the wall. The feces was so thick that it is still on the floor!

The dungeons have only one tiny window and no ventilation at all. In nauseating, vomit-inducing stench and unbearably suffocating humidity, millions of African men and boys were piled on top of one

**Male Slave Dungeons**

another like sardines for two weeks to three months at a time. They endured some of the most inhumane, evil treatment ever inflicted upon human beings. Fathers, brothers, and sons died on those floors.

## Female Slave Dungeons

We also stopped by the Female Slave Dungeon.

**Female Slave Dungeons**

It held about 500 female captives at a time. Women and girls were, like the males, held captive in dungeons. They too were given just enough water and food to stay alive. The dungeons had no ventilation, and the floors were covered with urine, feces and feminine waste.

Those women and girls weren't given anything to tend to their needs as females.

The purpose of enslaving women was for breeding more slaves. So British soldiers, who had left their wives in the U.K., entered the Female Dungeons nightly, scanned the room, selected whichever woman or girl they wanted, removed them from the dungeon raped them. If the women or girls became pregnant, they were moved to a home until they could give birth to, and care for, their mulatto (mixed) children. When the child was of age (about 9 or 10 years old), the soldiers would throw the women back in the dungeons and sell the children to the highest bidder in Palaver Hall. This happened to millions of women and children.

## The Cell

We also stopped by The Cell. Whenever a slave was disobedient or tried to resist a British soldier's commands, he or she would be placed in The Cell. British soldiers would carry slaves through three doorways, and throw them into the small dungeon. They then closed the three, thick, impenetrable doors behind them, locking the slave inside. Finally, because there was absolutely no air or ventilation in the hot, humid cell, the slaves would either starve to death or die from suffocation. The cell was used as a reminder to other slaves of hat could happen to anyone who disobeys their British masters.

## The Chapel

We also visited The Chapel. It was founded by The Society for the Propagation of the Gospel in Foreign Parts (SPG), which was a Church of England missionary organization. It was here that British Christians attended church, did their devotions, sang their hymns, worshipped,

**The Chapel**

read their bibles, preached a gospel that emphasized the importance of getting people saved so they could have eternal life.

What troubled my soul most is the church sits right on top of the Male Slave Dungeon. So while millions of black men and boys were crying out for help, for food, for water, gasping for air, suffering and dying in ankle-deep excrement, their British captors were attending church.

## Tunnel to the Slave Ships

**The Shrine**

In the last chamber of the male dungeons is a shrine. Behind the shrine, there used to be the entrance to a long tunnel (it was covered after the slave trade was officially abolished to symbolize the end of the Trans-Atlantic Slave Trade). When it was time for slaves to board ships, soldiers would bring slaves into this room, and separate the healthy from the sick. They would place the sick slaves in that room to the right of the shrine, where that small, dark opening is. There, in that room, they would throw sick human beings and leave them there until they died. The healthy ones would be sent into the tunnel that led to "The Door of No Return."

While I was standing in that room with my oldest son, I felt an indescribable sorrow in the depths of my soul. It was as though the misery and anguish and despair and fears and heartbreak and hopes of the millions of men and boys who suffered in that room had visited me. In a way that I cannot put into words, it felt like the spirits of people I knew were in that room. I was trying to keep from crying, so I kneeled down to change the lens on my camera. But every time I tried to open my camera backpack, I struggled to not break down in tears. But after a few moments, I just lost it. I wept for every man and boy who passed through those dungeons. I have never, ever felt so sad and indebted in my life! I kneeled in honor of every unspeakable evil they endured and just wept.

## The Door of No Return

When slave ships had arrived at the Cape Coast Castle, millions of men, women, boys, and girls were led from their dungeons through the Door of No Return. They boarded slave ships for the Americas, never to return. Here are some first-hand accounts of what happened to them on slave ships:

> "On the shelves below deck, that had four-foot room between them, the slaves lay chained two by two, in two rows under each other, on each side of the ship. They were pushed in so

The Door of No Return

tightly as books in a bookcase, I have seen a white man sent down to place them as advantageously as possible. I have seen them stowed so tight that no more could be pressed into the shelf. Every morning we found one living chained together with a dead."

Where slaves were loaded onto ships for
the Americas

James Barbot said, "It is very difficult for them [physicians] to work down below at the 'tween deck,' because of the tremendous heat down there. The air is so bad that the physicians faint and their light cannot burn."

John Newton, the man who was later converted to Christianity and who penned the song Amazing Grace, said captains and crew raped young African girls:

"When women and the girls were brought on board, naked and terrified, often exhausted from hunger and fatigue, they were exposed to pitiless mirth from the side of the white men. The Seamen shared the booty there and then in their fantasy, and each one reserved a girl for himself, till an opportunity would avail itself."

## The Elmina Castle

We also saw the Elmina Castle, which is not too far from the Cape Coast Castle. Most of the slaves who went to South America (mainly Brazil) suffered in and were transported on slave ships, from the Elmina Castle. Everything I shared about the Cape Coast Castle happened here but to millions of more people. What many people do not realize is that most slaves from Africa were sent to South America.

The Elmina Castle

## Why is This Significant?

I once took the class of a friendly, overall kind history professor who suggested that the European slave trade wasn't any worse than what black people were already doing to themselves in Africa. I explained that it is undeniable that slavery existed in Africa before Europeans arrived (Portuguese, Dutch, British, French); and, that slavery existed in Rome, Greece, and other ancient civilizations. However, also pointed out that there were significant differences between African slavery and European slavery.

According to Perbi, the author of *History of Indigenous Slavery in Ghana From the 15th to the 19th Century* (2004), in African societies, slaves were treated as housemaids by their owners and enjoyed privileges and had rights. Pawns (people who were presented as security for money borrowed), for example, gained their freedom after debts had been paid. They had the right to their names, could marry, own property, and give birth to children who were free (not considered as slaves). It was very difficult to identify such people as servants because they were protected, fed regularly and sheltered. They lived with their masters under the same roof and could progress from the status of a servant to a royal. A typical example was in the Niger Delta, where a servant could become the caretaker of the master's household and descendants of such a servant were considered royals. Female servants could marry those royals, and their children became royals as well.

African captives reduced to the status of slaves in European societies, on the contrary, were chattel, considered less human, unintelligent, and branded like cattle. On the plantations, they worked all year round whether sick, tired or weak and were regarded as a tool to be used and discarded when broken. Their names could be changed, and it was not a crime if anybody at all killed such a person. Children born of African and European parents were considered as slaves. While someone could argue that slavery in all its forms was terrible, I think it is important to note that there were significant differences between how Africans treated slaves and how Europeans treated them.

## Concluding Thoughts on Race

Although I have lived in a very racialized world my entire life, I had never thought very critically about it. I had never taken the time to study the history of the idea, and how it developed over the years. I always assumed that race was somehow real, and that it somehow helped us to understand people better. However, from my own experiences, my travels, and my studies, I have come to see that race and ethnicity are quite complex realities, and that power, money, status, freedom, education, and opportunities have historically been clustered together to privilege white people, and to exclude blacks and other people of color. In this chapter, I focused on the Trans-Atlantic Slave Trade, but I could have also focused on several other ethnicities who have suffered at the hands of system I just described.

Because race is so deeply ingrained in our understanding of ourselves and the world around us, my hope for this chapter is that you would begin thinking about it more intentionally and critically.

If you genuinely want to reach people in this increasingly diverse, multi-cultural, globalized world, I highly recommend you do a significant work of deconstructing how race has influenced your thoughts, attitudes, and actions. I also suggest you reconstruct your understanding of race so that you can have healthier, more informed interactions with others, especially people who do not share your color, ethnicity, or culture.

Often, people avoid talking about race because it is such an emotional issue. Indeed, there are very real racial divisions in America and around the world. I am not very optimistic about race-relations on a macro level. However, I have seen some powerful things happen in one-on-one relationships. So, to help reduce the racial tensions in our world, I recommend you start with you. Start by working to build relationships with co-workers and neighbors who do not share your race, ethnicity, or culture. Why not invite them to lunch or dinner? Why not try to learn about the stories of some of your co-workers or students.

I have discovered that it hard to hate or fear people when you are up close to them. Up close, fear fades and friendships form. Up close, in cordial conversation and exchanges, your perspective expands and you become more culturally self-aware, for it is through interacting with others that you learn how culturally different you are from them. Those realizations help you see more clearly that your "normal" is not normal to everyone else. That awareness is the foundation upon which you begin to develop intercultural competence. That is, through interacting with others, you will develop the awareness, the understanding, and, eventually, the skills to relate to others in ways that are deemed appropriate to them. We need a lot more interculturally competent people, of all ethnicities, in our world today. Why can't you be one of them?

# CHAPTER **TWELVE**

# BELIEFS

I have spent all this time talking about culture, personal experiences, personality, education, imagination, and race because I needed you to see how your belief system or frame of reference, and the frames of reference of your audiences, were shaped. I primarily wanted you to understand how your frame of reference determines what you see and how you see it. As such, regardless of who you think you see or what you know, it's essential for you to take a look at yourself, and be able to understand and describe the objective and subjective cultures to which you belong.

It is undeniable that your interpretive framework influences everything about you, and plays an integral part of how you teach, speak, or lead. Whenever you prepare a lesson or a presentation, your lesson or speech itself is unavoidably autobiographical because it reflects and reveals your frame of reference. However, without cultural self-awareness, your lessons or presentations will become nothing more than your own cultural values or preferences disguised with a veneer of objectivity. They will become nothing more than the transmission of culture- your culture to someone else.

However, in our multi-cultural, rapidly changing world, you can no longer assume that your listeners share, understand, or even appreciate your experiences. Nor can you assume that your experiences are (or should be) representative or normative.

To be sure, trying to understanding the objective and subjective cultures to which you belong is like a fish trying to become aware that is surrounded by water. It requires hard work.

Specifically, how can you develop cultural self-awareness? Based on my experiences in thousands of different contexts, and from a lot of reading, I believe you should read books that check and challenge your "normal." You should also immerse yourself in the daily lives of your listeners. You should reflect upon your immersion experiences through journaling, reflective paper assignments, or group reflections. Furthermore, you should conduct cultural self-studies in which you examine the beliefs, values, thought patterns, and pre-associations of your own culture.

Furthermore, while interacting with others through your immersion experiences, you should look for similarities and differences pertaining to the objective and subjective culture to which both you and the people you want to reach belong.

In addition to reflecting on the categories we have discussed thus far (power-distance, tolerance for ambiguity, individualism vs. collectivism, etc.), you should also reflect carefully on the following areas:

## Language, Dialect, and Communication

Language is a system of verbal and nonverbal symbols used to communicate. It has phonemes, morphemes, grammar, and syntax that form sentences. Words are merely signs that have no necessary connection to the things they reference, and sentences are groups of words arranged to express a complete thought.

What language do you speak? What dialect do you have? What words or phrases are unique to your culture? How does your language or dialect compare to the people around you? How might others interpret some of the words or phrases that you use?

Now consider the people you want to reach. What language/s or dialect/s do they speak? What are some keywords or phrases that they use?

Also, in your culture, do people communicate directly or indirectly? Do they have a high-context or low-context style of communication? How do people communicate non-verbally in your culture? How do they use their faces, hands, and bodies to communicate? How far apart do people stand from one another when they are talking?

What about the culture of the people you want to reach? How do they use words, sounds, facial expressions, body language, or space to communicate with each other?

## Social Structure

Every society ranks categories of people in a hierarchy. People with power, money, and prestige are at the top of the hierarchy, and those without power, money, and prestige are at the bottom of it. There are vast inequalities of power, wealth, and prestige when it comes to race, ethnicity, and class. Inequality refers no only to the current finances of people but also refers to the differential access to valuable resources that could help them get power, wealth, and prestige.

With that in mind, how are power, money, and prestige distributed in your neighborhood or city? Which ethnic groups are at the top of the hierarchy? Which ones are in the middle, and which ones are at the bottom? How did things get structured that way? Who has the power in your city and how did they get it? Who has the wealth in your town and how did they get it? Also, where on the social hierarchy in your city are you and your family situated?

Now consider the people you want to reach. Where do they fall on the social hierarchy? How much access have they had to resources that could help them get power, wealth, and prestige? Has the access been fair or differential?

## Power

Power is the ability to influence or control behavior, and authority is the right to exercise power over others. According to anthropologists and political scientists, there is coercive power, persuasive power, and hegemonic power. In day-to-day life, there are positive and negative sanctions that guide behavior. Formal sanctions are official rewards to either encourage desirable behaviors or punishments to discourage the breaking of rules. Informal sanctions are designed to do the same thing, to influence the behavior of people.

Power gets organized into political systems that guide societies. There are bands and tribes, which are decentralized systems of political organizations. There are kingdoms, which are centralized systems of political organizations with inheritable leadership positions, usually passed down through families. Then, there are states, which are highly centralized systems of political organization in which power resides in institutions and offices.

What formal or informal positive sanctions exist in your culture? That is, what behaviors or beliefs are rewarded in your culture? Who is in charge of distributing those rewards? Specifically, how are those rewards distributed?

What formal or informal negative sanctions exist in your culture. In other words, which behaviors or beliefs get punished? Who enforces the punishments? Specifically, how do people implement the sanctions?

What about the people you want to reach? What are some of the formal or informal sanctions of their cultures? What gets rewarded and what gets punished? Who has the power to distribute those rewards, and who has the authority to enforce the negative sanctions?

How does your culture's understanding and use of power compare to the culture of the people you want to reach?

## Ethnicity

Ethnicity refers to the set of cultural ideas held by an ethnic group that has a shared history, language, customs, and traditional beliefs. What is the shared history of your ethnic group? What are some of your ethnic group's customs and traditional beliefs? How do people in your ethnic group dress, greet one another, or eat? What is considered a snack in your ethnic group? Do you eat cookies, crackers, or crickets for a snack? Tarantulas? Do you eat pigeons, cats, dogs, or snakes?

What is the ethnicity of people you want to reach? What is their shared story that unites them? What are some of their customs, cultural artifacts, or songs? What foods or snacks do they eat? What music do they like?

How does your ethnicity compare to theirs regarding history, language, customs, and beliefs?

## Sex, Sexuality, and Gender

You also want to reflect on sex, sexuality, and gender roles. Sex is biological, and gender is a social construct. Gender refers to expectations of roles played by males and females. Those expectations are culturally defined, not biological. According to anthropologists, in some cultures gender is fluid.

For example, Egypt is a male-centered place. According to custom and culture, the woman's place is in the home. Most women in Egypt, I'm told by men and from books, take pride in having children and keeping a house well. The men are the primary breadwinners, and even do jobs usually dominated by women. The men in Egypt are housekeepers, flight attendants, and waiters. In fact, I don't think I saw one female waiter or housekeeper.

Because of this male-centered norm, the men and women almost always talked to me, even after they knew my wife had made all the reservations, travel arrangements, and had all the documents neatly for our trip.

In your culture, what is the role of men? What is the role of boys? What is the role of women? Of girls? In your culture, who is the head of your household? Men or women?

What about the culture of the people you want to reach? In their cultures, what are the roles of men, boys, women, and girls? How do those roles compare to your culture's gender roles?

Also, how is sexuality viewed in your culture? What is considered sexually inappropriate? How do your culture's views about sexuality compare to the views of the people you want to reach?

## Systems of Production and Exchange

There are four broad systems of production and three systems of exchange that societies everywhere use. Regarding systems of production, some cultures survive by gathering wild plants and hunting animals. Other cultures cultivate wild and domesticated plants to survive. Also, some cultures use domesticated animals to survive, while different cultures intensely and constantly cultivate plants on permanent fields.

Concerning systems of exchange, some cultures exchange goods using a system of generalized reciprocity, balanced reciprocity, or negative reciprocity. In cultures that practice generalized reciprocity, people give goods or services to others in their culture without any attempt at determining the value of those goods or services, and without any specific expectations about how and when those goods or services should be returned. In cultures that practice balanced reciprocity, people exchange equivalent goods or services. In cultures that practice negative reciprocity, both people involved in an exchange try to get more than they give.

In addition to using a system of reciprocity, some cultures use a system of redistribution in which a centralized authority collects goods and services and distributes them to others. Taxes are a form of redistribution.

Third, some societies have a market economy, which is a system of exchange in which individuals exchange their physical or intellectual labor for money. They then use that money to acquire goods and services.

Some economic theories believe that every group of people wants the same things, regardless of their particular situations, and that they seek to get those things in the same ways as every other culture. I and others believe that economic behavior and motivations vary by culture. That is, economic behavior, with relation to how people produce, exchange, and consume goods and use services depends on their unique cultural (personal, political, economic, religious, and spiritual) contexts.

In any case, how do people in your culture produce, exchange, and consume goods and use services? How do people in the culture you want to reach product, exchange, and consume goods and use services? How do your culture's systems of production and exchange compare to the people you want to reach?

## Kinship and Marriage

You want to also reflect on your own culture's beliefs and assumptions about kinship and marriage. In some places, one's status is based on one's kinship. There are two ways to determine who are one's relatives: descent and marriage.

Descent can be seen as unilineal or cognatic. Unilineal descent traces relatedness exclusively or predominantly through one parent. There are three types of unilinear descent: patrilineal, matrilineal, and dual descent. In patrilineal descent, people trace their kinship through the male line. In matrilinial descent, people trace their lineage through the female line. In dual descent, people trace their lineage through both their fathers' and mothers' lines.

In cultures subscribe to cognatic descent, people trace their lineage through both maternal and paternal ancestors. There are two types cognatic descent: bilateral and ambilinial. In bilateral descent, kinship is traced through both the mother's and the father's lines. In ambilineal descent, people choose their lineage upon reaching adulthood.

In some cultures, your kinship is determined by who you marry. In some contexts, marriage is ceremony in which two people who love each other publicly declare their commitment to one another. In other cultures, marriage is a publicly recognized social or legal union that creates a socially sanctioned context for sexual intimacy. However, in some cultures, marriage is a political, economic, and social act that connects two families and helps to bring financial security and political alliances. That is, marriage is a means to help a family acquire wealth, power, and prestige.

Furthermore, in some cultures, marriage is also important because it can help continue a person's lineage by producing children. In that sense, marriage is not just personal, but also a social, political, and economic.

In your culture, how is kinship decided? Do you trace your lineage through your father's line, your mother's line, or both? Do you have the freedom to choose your kinship upon reaching adulthood?

Also, how is marriage viewed in your culture? Is it something that unites two people who are in love, is it a social, political, and economic act, or is it something else entirely? How are marriage ceremonies conducted in your culture? And, how do your culture's assumptions, beliefs, and behaviors about kinship and marriage compare to the assumptions and beliefs of the culture of the people you would like to reach?

## Religion

You need to also reflect on your culture's assumptions and beliefs about religion. Religion is a cultural system of symbols. Those symbols get organized to invoke emotion and to educate people. When symbols get arranged into a system, they become rituals, which are just patterned, repeated, predictable actions. Symbols and rituals only have meaning to people within a culture when those symbols and rituals are viewed in light of larger stories or meta-narratives that they believe is significant.

All of the following religions have symbols, rituals, and stories: Christianity, Judaism, Catholicism, Islam, Zoroastrianism, Native American Religion, Traditional African Religion, Chinese Popular Religion, Shinto, Hinduism, Buddhism, Jainism, Baha'i, and Sikhism.

What religion, if any, do you, your family, or your culture practice? What are the religious symbols, rituals, and stories of your religion? How do your religious assumptions, beliefs, and practices compare to the assumptions, beliefs, and practices of the people you want to reach?

Even if you are agnostic or an atheist, it is important for you to understand how your beliefs and assumptions compare or contrast to the religious beliefs and assumptions of the people you want to reach.

## Globalization

Globalization is the integration of local, regional, and/or national production, exchange, and culture into a global system. It is marked by multi-directional flows of goods and services, people and information. It is rooted in colonialism when European countries either replaced or infused their values on conquered territories. They created a colonial hegemony in those areas. Post-colonialism and neocolonialism persisted because of the legacy of colonialism.

However, people resisted, collectively and individually, to create a counter-hegemony. Some have worked to decolonize themselves, and localize, resignify and reinterpret, or remove altogether, the ideas, practices, cultures, and values of colonial oppressors.

At this point in history, industrialized nations at the core of globalization benefit tremendously from it while agricultural, non-industrial countries—those on the periphery—are dependent on industrialized nations, and are being excluded from economic development.

How have you or your culture benefited or suffered from colonialism or globalization? How have the people you want to reach benefited or suffered from colonialism or globalization?

## Final Thoughts on Cultural Self-Awareness

The study of objective culture as described above should lead you to gain a more clear understanding of the subjective aspects of your culture as well as the cultures of others. That is, your immersion experiences in the cultures of other people should help you understand the beliefs, values, assumptions, and feelings of the people you serve.

By immersing yourself in the daily lives of your listeners, you will learn about others while simultaneously becoming aware of how culturally-near, or culturally-distant, you are in relation to others. Immersing yourself into the culture of others allows you to not only look through a window into the lives of others, but it also gives you a mirror in which to see yourself more clearly. That reflective immersion and critical self-study will help you become more culturally self-aware.

What should you do with your new self-awareness? First, I recommend you identify anything in your frame of reference that might be getting in the way of you reaching underperforming, sad, troubled, fragile or hurting people.

Second, you should try your best to correct those beliefs, assumptions, and behaviors. Do you have any any tacit ethnocentricity or pride in you that makes you feel that your culture is better than the culture of the people you want to help? Furthermore, is anything in your past-any accomplishment, any accolade, any superlatives, any trophies, any championships, or anything else that could make you feel like you are inherently a better person than others? If so, I cannot stress strongly enough that you need to work to remove that belief immediately because it will hinder your work with others.

In place of your pride or tacit ethnocentricity, I suggest you take an honest assessment of yourself and realize that, on a human level, you are not inherently better than the person or people you would like to reach. Yes, your circumstances may be much better, but your circumstances do not make you inherently better.

You need to look at the person that you're trying to help as someone who is not much different from you. You need to see him or her as a human being. Like you, they want to be happy. Like you, they want to experience joy. Like you, they want to experience peace. Like you, they have dreams too.

I believe that if you had been given the circumstances that the person you're trying to reach has been given, you probably would be in the same situation as that person. So, the first thing you need to do is to understand that the person you are trying to reach is just like you on a basic human level.

Sometimes I hear people have conversations about nature versus nurture—about whether one's behavior is determined by one's biology or by one's circumstances. I am convinced it is a both-and answer. That is, I believe we are shaped by our biology and our environment. If that is the case, then you need to recognize that the people you are trying to reach have been given circumstances that have influenced them to make decisions, which, in turn, have put them in their current situations.

All this is to say, never allow yourself to become the kind of person who feels that you are better than other people, period. Never allow yourself to become the kind of person who has to boast about all of your accomplishments to make yourself feel you better than them. If you find you are always talking to others about your accomplishments or the superiority of the way you or your culture do things, then chances are you have some pride or insecurity in your heart that you need to address.

A proverb says, "like clouds and winds without rain is a man who boasts of gifts he doesn't have." A person who boasts, in other words, is empty. People who boast are all air.

Instead of puffing yourself up, humble yourself, and work to become the kind of person who is culturally self-aware, who understands the cultures of others, and who has the skills to relate to people across cultural lines in ways that make them feel honored, valued, respected, and loved. If you do that, you will become interculturally proficient, and REACH a lot more people.

# R.E.A.C.H.

# R.E.A.C.H.

## PART 2

# R.E.A.C.H.

U P TO THIS POINT IN THE BOOK, I have been laying the foundation for reaching others. For years, I used to jump right into the R.E.A.C.H. approach without ever examining the significance of one's frame of reference. However, through trial-and-error, I realized that before we begin reaching others, we need to take a careful look at ourselves.

Now that we have done the hard work of examining ourselves, we can turn to reaching others. R.E.A.C.H. approach.

Naturally, I call it the R.E.A.C.H. method because it spells the word REACH:
R stands for RELATIONSHIPS.
E stands for ENGAGEMENT
A stands for AWARENESS
C stands for CONVINCE
H stands for HAND

In chapter thirteen, I write about relationships. I am convinced everything we hope to accomplish must pass through the door of relationships. We have to build healthy relationships with people if we are going to help them create lasting changes in their lives. Those relationships can be short-term or long-term, but they must healthy, and they must be real.

Even if you are not naturally a relational person, or if you are an introvert, how can you cultivate a healthy relationship with someone that results in positive changes in their lives? In that chapter, I share ten proven principles you can begin applying immediately and begin improving the quality of every relationship you have. When I lead my seminar, R.E.A.C.H., my discussions on relationships alone often takes almost two hours. I have had so many people thank me just for the information I share in that chapter alone.

In chapters fourteen and fifteen I write about ENGAGEMENT. We must engage people in novel, positive, unexpected ways by building culturally relevant bridges between our content and their contexts. I share with you activities and questions so that we can learn about who they are, and assess their needs, identify their imbalances, learn about where they are from, find out their strengths and their areas of growth. It is crucial for us to engage them on their levels. In that chapter, I also share ways to capture and keep the attention of any person or audience you are trying to reach.

In chapter sixteen, I write about AWARENESS. In that chapter, I talk about how and why people change. They do not change because we think they have issues. They change when they realize they have issues. More specifically, people change when they become painfully aware of the imbalances in their lives. As such, I argue that we have to help them become painfully aware of the imbalances in their lives. I share with you some things that I have seen work powerfully in the lives of others and helped them become aware of their need to change. This is really important! I will spend a good deal of time exploring this more fully.

In chapter seventeen, I write about the C of REACH, which stands for CONVINCE. Only after people become aware of their need to change are they open to be convinced that you have what they need. We have to convince people that they are more significant than their circumstances by giving them glimpses of their own possibilities. I have some important ideas about how to do that. For now, just know that if you want to reach anyone, you must help them imagine themselves succeeding in school, work, relationships, or life.

Then, in chapter eighteen, I write about the H, which stands for HAND. To reach people, we have to extend our hand, literally or figuratively (ideally both), and walk with people, and empower them to make decisions that can change the quality of their lives forever. Change begins when people make decisions. We can literally reach our hand and shake on decisions that people make. Or, we can figuratively reach out our hand and walk with them on their journey to realizing their potential. I will share with you several practical ways to reach out your hand in that chapter.

———

CHAPTER **THIRTEEN**

# RELATIONSHIPS

Let us go back to the point in my story that I began sharing with you in the first chapter of this book. Do you remember that young man—the younger, troubled version of me—who was sitting on a park bench? The young man who had just dropped out of high school and who was probably going to do something that resulted in him getting locked up or killed- do you remember him? That was me. It was really me. No exaggeration. I was in a very dark situation. Now imagine you are walking by that young man on that park bench. What do you think needed to be done first to reach me?

I am absolutely convinced that the very first thing you need to do to reach anyone is to try to build a relationship with them. Without a healthy relationship, you will limit your effectiveness as a leader or a teacher. The maxim is true, people do not care how much you know until they know how much you care. You show you care by building a healthy relationship with people.

Everything you hope to accomplish with others—improved grades, behavior, classroom management, office morale, parental involvement, test scores—should pass through the door of relationships. I have seen apathetic, angry people turn things around after I was able to establish relationships with them. Yes, relationships really matter. It is sad that I have to say that, but I am hearing more and more people who have been told by their bosses that relationships are overrated. After hearing me speak, they thank me for reaffirming their belief in the power and importance of building relationships.

To be sure, I do not believe you can relationship your way to academic, personal, or business success. You just can't relationship your way there. However, you cannot succeed in the grand scheme of things without relationships. I don't think you should end at relationship-building, but I do contend you should start there.

That being said, it is easier to build a relationship with people who are just like you, who share your culture, values, and worldview. But how do you build one with people who are not like you, who do not look like you, believe like you, or behave like you?

This is important because, as I have mentioned already, our world is rapidly changing. It is changing in terms of population density, technology, travel, immigration patterns, and growing in ethnic, religious, political, and socio-economic diversity. These changes have created a world that requires us to interact with students and families of different cultural origins regularly—be they in our classrooms, our schools, next door, across town, our thousands of miles away. Whether or not you embrace these changes, they will continue to increase in both frequency and intensity and grow in importance.

However, most people no longer find it necessary to seek compromises with people who have perceptions, opinions, and attitudes different from their own. As a result, more of us are segregating ourselves into communities, and clubs where we are surrounded by people who think the way we do. The problem with this is it is leading to more misunderstanding, more polarization, more intolerance, and is creating a lot of chaos. If this trend continues, we will be seeing more school shootings, more terrorist attacks, and a lot more darkness in our world. Sadly, I do not believe we can arrest our way out of this problem. The darkness and divisions and despair are too deep and wide and pervasive. Rather than cursing this darkness, we must find ways to be a light. We must find ways to reach people who are different from us.

The most important way to do that, I argue, is for you to build relationships with people, especially people who are different from you.

What I share with you in this chapter works across culture, divides, and across religions.

My eleventh-grade English teacher, Erin Gruwell, who came from an upper-middle-class family, came into my classroom full of students Blacks, Latinos, Asians, and several Caucasian students. Culturally and socioeconomically, she was worlds apart from us, and yet she was still able to reach many of us because she knew how to build relationships with us.

If you want to work well cross-culturally, the most important thing is not technical skills. Rather, you need to know how to make a friend. You need to know how to build relationships. You need to know how to enter into someone's life so they feel they can trust you. I'm going to share with you what I call the road to real relationships.

# OPENNESS

I think we start off in life with an openness toward life. We are open to new people, and open to new experiences, and open to the adventure that life has to offer. But then "life happens," and begins to make us close ourselves off from the world around us. Maybe we get our feelings hurt, or someone bullies us at school, or someone attacks our character, or talks about us behind our back. Maybe someone complained about something you said or did. Or, maybe you received a bad job review, or lost a job, or made a mistake that damaged your reputation. Whatever it is, there is a tendency among many people to cross their arms, and close themselves off from being open, vulnerable, or receptive to things and people that are new and different.

However, the people that changed my life are those who embodied openness in the best way. My former professor, Dr. Elmer once said,

"Openness is the ability to welcome people into your presence so that they feel safe and secure." The word hospitality it has the same root as the word hospital, and when you go to a hospital, what are you looking for? You're looking to be made well; you're looking for healing. In the same way, I believe when you extend hospitality to someone, you help them heal.

Openness is the ability to have a posture about you, to have a demeanor about you, that makes others feel safe and secure. When you embody openness, your eyes smile when you see someone. When people come into your presence, your warmth lifts their spirits. People feel safe and secure when they can see, in your eyes, that you are happy to see them.

I had teachers come into my life, who, when I walked into their presence, they were so open, so loving, and so welcoming that I enjoyed being around them. Whenever I got close to them, they would greet me with such warmth and kindness. They greeted me in such a way that I sometimes felt myself begin to heal emotionally.

It was weird. Something inside me began to heal by the way these people treated me, by the way they welcomed me into their presence. When I walked into their classrooms, they were happy to see me. When I walked into their offices, they were there to greet me with a warm smile, a pat on the back, and a smile in their eyes.

I met a teacher in Columbia, South Carolina, who said that she had been having problems with the lunch lady of the school but did not know why. After talking to the lunch lady and a few trusted friends, and she concluded that he was coming off as a rude and mean person, even though she was not aware of it. She identified herself as an introvert and realized that others perceived her introversion as rude, distant, and unfriendly. That epiphany to her forced her to work on becoming more open to others.

Do you come off as open to others? Or, do you come off as someone who is rude, abrasive, or cold? It would not hurt (well, maybe a little) to ask some people whose opinion you value how you come off to others. Then hear with an open heart what they have to say about their perceptions of you. Their observations could help you to grow.

Another teacher I met recently told me that she had been feeling down, drained, and depressed. She said that it was sapping her of her joy, and robbing her of her motivation to teach. Then one day she decided that she was going change her attitude about her job. She said that she decided that she was going to greet each day with love in her heart, and gratitude for the little things. That little shift altered everything for her. She said she now walks onto campus more open, enthusiastic, and ready to learn and teach.

Dr. Robert Long, a pastor in Oklahoma City, is a perfect example of what it means to embody openness. I did an internship at his church several years ago and spent a good deal of time with Dr. Long. Whenever I saw him in person or talked with him on the phone, he greeted me in the most enthusiastic, spirit-lifting way. He would say, with the biggest smile on his face, and joy in his eyes, "MANNY!!!!" No matter how low I might have been feeling, his presence always had a way of bringing me joy.

One of the most important ways to practice openness is to be the host and not just a guest.

What about you? Can you welcome someone into your presence with openness so that they feel secure, safe, and uplifted? Do you greet people in a way that helps them feel that they do not have to watch their backs? To be sure, I am not saying you need to have unbridled enthusiasm and contagious optimism (even those things are not bad). All I am recommending is that you work on greeting the people you meet with more openness.

I'll be the first to admit that embodying openness is not always an easy thing to do. Sometimes with all of the administrative work that you have to do, and the lesson plans that you need to prepare, and other demands related to running a business, it is very hard to practice openness.

The fact is, sometimes we are just too busy to be open. The problem with being too busy, however, is that it might cause you to miss an opportunity to make a big difference in someone's life. Busy-ness prevents you from embodying open-ness.

But because openness is a prerequisite to reaching anyone, you must work on becoming less busy. You must manage your time more carefully. Do whatever you need to do become more emotionally and mentally available to new people, information, and situations. That.

Finally, I need to remind you that you can make people feel welcome or unwelcome, included or excluded, loved or tolerated without saying a word. Your facial expressions, body language, and behavior can be quite useful in making people feel at ease in your presence, room, school, building, office, or meeting.

## ACCEPTANCE

In addition to openness, I highly recommend you work to develop acceptance of others. Now let me be clear, when I call you to embody acceptance, I am not saying you need to condone or celebrate everyone's choices and lifestyles. In fact, I think that kind of acceptance is un-livable and disingenuous.

By acceptance, I am referring the ability to continue holding people in high regard, continuing to see beauty, potential, value, and worth, even though you see their "issues." It means being able to continue holding someone in high regard even though you see their low estate. It's your ability to continue venerating someone even though you see their issues; it's the ability to continue seeing potential even though you see a lot of problems. I'll admit to you that it is tough to embody acceptance.

Where I'm from, having lived in thirty-eight places, I've learned that most people love you until they know you. People will love you when you are dressed up, and when you are paying for their meals. They love you when you agree with them. They love you when you meet their standards. However, when people see the defective parts of you—your character flaws, and your brokenness, and your bad attitude, or your insecurities, and your shortcomings—they usually distance themselves from you. More often than not, when people see your issues, they stop loving you. They love you until they know you, but once they know you- more often than not-they stop loving you.

However, those who have changed my life are those who saw my issues and insecurities and inadequacies but did not give up on me. They did not act as though my issues were invisible, or that they did not exist. Instead, they saw my issues, but they also saw past my issues. They looked past my issues and saw something more significant. They saw that I did not know how to study, but they also saw a college graduate. They noticed that I had a bad temper, but they also saw someone who could one day have peace. They someone who had several character flaws, and they also saw someone who could achieve great things. They saw my problems but did not hold them against me. Instead, they saw my potential and kept calling me up to it. They accepted me.

Acceptance is critical if you're going to reach people. If you're going to build a relationship with anyone, you have to work to focus on their potential, even though you see their problems. It is the ability to continue venerating someone when you could just as well vilify them. It's the ability to see someone's worth even though you have a whole lot of reasons to see what's wrong. It's the ability to continue loving someone even though they may not have done anything to really deserve it. Can you love someone whose behavior you do not like? Can you accept someone who has bad habits? When that young person comes into your classroom with a bad attitude and doesn't want to talk to you, can you still see worth? Can you accept the young person who has his head down on his desk- the one who didn't do his homework, who maybe got into a fight the day before?

A kindergarten teacher told me a story of one of her kids who had a lot of issues. One morning, when she greeted him as he walked into class, he lashed out at her, saying, "You're ugly, you're stupid, and you're fat." She responded, saying, "Sounds like somebody needs a hug! Come here!" And she commenced to squeeze him. That's what acceptance looks like.

My friend, practicing acceptance, or tolerance, is not easy to do. But let me just free you up just in case you don't know this- the person wearing your clothes right now, reading these words right now, has some issues. Sorry to burst your bubble, but we all have some issues. We all have some shortcomings. We all have some character flaws.

So, with your issues, can you give the people you work with permission to have issues? Can you give the people you work with permission to have issues? Can you give them permission to have some brokenness in their lives? Can you give your colleagues permission to be imperfect? What about your supervisor? Can they have issues? The better you are able to embody acceptance, the better your chances of reaching them will be.

Your practicing of acceptance will open so many doors for you. Loving others when they feel unloveable will break down so many barriers for you. Your acceptance, your love for them, will surprise them. It will shock them. They'll wonder, "Why is this person treating me this way?" "Why are they still nice to me even though I've done everything in my power to get this person out of my face?" "Why does this person still go out of his way to let me know that he cares about me?" "Why does this person keep encouraging me, even though I have not demonstrated that I am willing to work hard? Why?"

The more you practice acceptance, the less others will understand why you are still working with them- which is precisely what you want. Your love for them allows you to say, "Yes, I see your brokenness. Yes, I see your shortcomings. Yes, I see your character flaws. Yes, I know your mother said you weren't going to be anybody. But I see something great in you. Yes, I know your father has been gone, and you do not know what it means to be a man? Yes, I know that you have been irresponsible. But I still love you and believe in you. Yes, I understand that some things happened to you in your life that hurt you, but I still see a high school graduate. I see a doctor. I see a lawyer. I see a teacher. I still see someone who can be happily married. I see someone who can one day be a great father or mother. I see someone who can make a big difference in this world." That's what acceptance looks and sounds like in real life. When you speak those things into the lives of people who are living beneath their potential, you will encourage them in wonderful ways.

# TRUST

I have felt betrayed or abandoned so many times in my life that my heart became so sore that it could not bear the touch of being hurt by anyone else. To protect myself, I put up emotional walls to keep people from getting close to me. I let them get close enough to feel connected, but not so close that they could hurt me. To get me to let down my walls, several people had to work to get me to trust them.

To build a healthy relationship with the people you want to reach, you need to learn how to develop trust. Trust is the ability to build confidence in the relationships so that both parties believe the other will not intentionally injure them, but, in fact, act in the other's best interest.

The foundation of every relationship is trust. If you do not have trust, if you can't earn someone's trust, they will never allow you to get close enough to them to reach them. They will never allow you to speak things into their lives because they will always question your motives. They'll always question your agenda. Trust is the ability to make someone feel as though you really care about them, and that you want what is best for them, and not just what's best for you.

I met a teacher who baked one of her students a birthday cake for his birthday and gave it to him. Surprised, he thanked her and walked away with his cake. Two or three days later, she saw him at his locker. She also noticed in his locker was the birthday cake she had given him. It was uneaten. He hadn't touched it. Surprised, she asked him why he hadn't eaten it. He told her that no one had ever given him a birthday cake, and he didn't want to ruin it. That teacher's little act of generosity went a long way with that student. She said that he went from the bottom of her class to the top. His grades went up, his behavior improved, and he also became her protector. She said, "When new kids were giving me a hard time, I wouldn't have to say anything to them because he would check them for me." When you build trust with your students, they stand up for you.

I met another teacher who was about seventy years old, and who had a fantastic impact on his kids. When I asked him to reveal his secret to me, he said that he picked one or two students a day to privately encourage. He wrote them little notes, and gave them little gifts, or spent a little extra time speaking to them about non-academic subjects. He told me, "Manny, my wife died recently, and I don't know how much longer I have to live. But with the time I have left, I just want these kids to know that I care about them, that they matter to me, that

I love them." That man's students loved him. They trusted him. It was a beautiful thing to see. That teacher's little acts of kindness had a big impact on his kids and on me.

What are some things you can do to build that kind of trust with others? It won't happen by accident. You have to be intentional about it.

# LEARNING

Next on the road to developing healthy relationships is learning. If people trust you, you can then begin learning things about them, learning from them, and learning with them. Those are at least three levels of learning. When you walk into a classroom of strangers, and you're the teacher, it is your job to influence them. It's your job to affect change in their lives.

As such, you would do well to become students of that group of people. You would do well to become an anthropologist of them and their cultures. I spent a great deal of time in the first part of the book talking about your frame of reference, so I will not spend much more time here talking about the things you need to learn.

All I will say is that you would do well to find out whom your students want to emulate. You would do well to learn about their music. Who are their role models? Who do they look up to? Why do they dress that way? How do they dress, why are they wearing those pants? Why are some wearing Cortez Nikes? Why are some wearing Dickies? Why are some sagging their pants? Why are some wearing extra large white T-shirts? Why are some wearing wave caps? Why are some wearing gold teeth and silver teeth in their mouths? Why do they have tattoos, and what do they mean? What are they trying to tell you about who they are, and how they see themselves, and what they value? What music are they listening to? What are they internalizing?

What are they are imbibing? What are they reading? Which magazines? Which websites are they visiting? What are they posting on Facebook? On Twitter? Instagram? What about Pinterest? Snapchat?

Become a student of your students. Trust me, studying your students or audiences will be very useful for you when I discuss engagement in the next chapter.

But right now, you need to learn about them from afar. Just observe people. Then, if you are embodying openness and acceptance, they will let you in, and eventually, you'll start learning from them. They'll tell you things that they usually don't tell adults. They'll start sharing secrets with you. You'll begin learning more deeply, more carefully, more personally about them.

There's a story of some young ladies. I think they were in Florida, I do not remember the state, but they were wearing all of these colorful shoestrings. Eventually, a teacher was able to earn the trust of one of the young ladies in her school, and the teacher asked about the meaning of the girls wearing colorful shoestrings. Was it just a fad? Or was there something more going on? The teacher found out that the shoestrings were really a menu to let them know what the girls were willing to do sexually.

The teacher was blown away, and eventually, that teacher had to share that information with the leadership of the school. What do you think the school district did? No more colorful shoestrings! What do you think the young ladies, the girls, did? Initially, they complied. However, a little bit later, after the paranoia had died down, the girls started wearing little bracelets and wristbands, and they began communicating another way. You see, young people today and young people in every generation, speak another language. It's almost like the dog whistle—when humans blow a dog whistle we as human beings can't hear it, but the dogs can hear it quite well. Now

I am not saying that children are dogs; my point is merely that they have another language.

In one school, rubber bands in the girls' hair are a menu for the boys to let them know what the girls are willing to do sexually. That is happening in middle schools!

Is it possible that the young people around you are speaking another language that you can't hear? Every day, they might be communicating with one another—expressing values and their visions and things that are important to them that we can't hear. Through their clothes, tattoos, piercings, music, art, poetry and other aspects of their objective cultures, they are communicating things. You will only learn what they are saying if you become a student of them.

Establishing rapport with them, learning about them and then learning from them are the first two levels of learning. Eventually, you will learn with them. That is the third level of learning.

If you stop learning today, you should stop leading, speaking, or teaching tomorrow. You might as well quit because you will eventually become irrelevant. You will lose influence, and you will become outdated. Some of your techniques and methodologies will no longer be relevant to the people you want to help. Love people enough to keep learning about them.

There are times when I feel I am getting out of touch with some of my audiences. To correct this, I take off my teacher hat and become a student again. Staying close to the people I am trying to reach has taught me so much about myself and others. In fact, a lot of what I know has just come from me learning about them from afar, learning from them up close, and learning with them, together.

Fortunately, I've made a lot of great connections with people. Many of them trust me and share things with me that they don't even share with their best friends. I'd like to think that they do so because I've humbled myself to learn about them, and I consistently do my best to let them know I care.

# UNDERSTANDING

If you want to develop a real relationship with someone, you will eventually need to get to a place of understanding. If you are open and accepting; if you're developing trust and learning about, from, and with them, eventually you will begin to understand them.

But what is understanding? It is merely the ability to see patterns of behavior and the underlying values and assumptions that reveal the integrated wholeness and integrity of a person and a people. In other words, understanding gives you a sense of the tapestry of a group of people. It gives you a sense of their pulsating core. It gives you a sense of their values.

In every culture, there are unspoken rules. Insiders know them; outsiders don't. There are certain ways you carry yourself when you go to specific neighborhoods. There are certain things you talk about, and certain things you don't. That kind of knowledge comes only when you achieve understanding.

How well do you understand the people with whom you work? Why do they talk about certain things in the way they do? Why are they reticent about other topics? Gaining an understanding about their patterns of thinking, feeling and behaving is vital.

# COMPETENCE

I think you also need to develop competence. Competence is the ability to conduct a task well, and have others believe in your ability to conduct a task well. There are two types of competences: there is competence by power and there is competence by information.

Competence by power simply says, "I have the title, I was assigned, I am in charge, someone appointed me, I'm the boss, and people will follow me because I'm in charge." People may follow you because you have the title, but they will never respect you as a person. If you only have competence by power, once you leave the room, your influence goes with you. They talk about you behind your back.

Then there is competence by information. Competence by information is when people respect you because you have information that is relevant to them. When you have this kind of competence, your persuasive capital grows tremendously.

In other words, you know some things and be able to do some things that can help others. You become competent when you can do something that others need done, or have insight that others lack.

Many leaders fail to connect with people because they lean too much on their titles. However, it is not until people see you have competence by information that you will have a shot at reaching them.

For example, whenever I speak anywhere, I work very hard to demonstrate that I have competence by information. That is, I know things that can really add value to my audience's lives.

## COMMONALITY

Another essential characteristic on the road to developing real relationships is commonality. Commonality is just another way of saying you have to have the ability to give the person with whom you are speaking the perception that you have a common goal with that person.

If you're going to develop a healthy, meaningful relationship with someone, you need to have a mutual trust, and the other person has to believe that you both want the same things.

For example, as a leader, there is nothing wrong with you pulling aside an underperforming person and saying, "Hey, what's going on? You okay? What's the problem?" Regardless of what they say, it is helpful just to let them know, "Look, I'm on your team. I got your back. I want you to do well. You don't have to fight me. You don't. I'm on your team, I want the same things you want. I want you to be happy. I want you to be successful. I want you to go and do great things. I want you to be fulfilled. We want the same things. Let's work together." When someone connects with you like that, it makes a big difference.

I will never forget when a close friend of mine was given an opportunity to give himself a grade in our class, and he gave himself an F. My teacher pulled him aside, and did precisely what I mentioned above, except with a little more fire, and a few more words I dare not include here.

My teacher challenged him and let him know that she was on his team. It made such a difference in him that he went on to become a very influential person on campus. All of us guys wanted to be just like him.

When a person hears you say things like, "Other people may have given up on you, but I have not given up on you. I want the same things you want for yourself. I want you to be happy, but you gotta work with me." I have used this several times with people, and it has been effective.

People often thank me for the little time I give them after my speeches. I was recently in Texas when a line of 800 or 900 people waited to speak with me. It took me over two hours to talk to everyone. I finished my presentation at 2:45 in the afternoon, but I did not leave the school until 6 PM. As is often the case, those young people shared some of their deepest, most painful secrets with me. Then often ask me for advice about something going on in their lives.

I have found it extremely helpful to make sure people know that I want the best for them. If I sense some resistance to what I am saying to them, I stop and say, "Hey, I want you to be happy. I want you to be successful. Now hear me out. I'm on your team." They often soften up a little after that and realize that I do not personally benefit from what I'm telling them. People in general listen a bit better when they believe the advice is coming from someone who wants for them what they want for themselves.

# CHARISMA

It would help if you also develop charisma. Charisma is the ability to inspire people with information that solves their significant problems. For example, you might go into a community that is experiencing some kind of substantial issues. Maybe it is a recession. Perhaps it is high unemployment. Or perhaps there is a drought. Maybe there is a high dropout rate or a high teen pregnancy rate.

Whatever the case, whenever you go into a place where people are distressed, hurting, and discouraged, those people are searching for answers. Many of them are scraping their existence for hope, and it is in that context that a leader often emerges. Someone rises up and shares a vision that he or she believes can solve their problem(s).

That leader shares her heart, shares her strategy, and shares her mission. If people believe in that vision, they galvanize around it. They support the person who has the vision and plan to help them.

In the same way, if you are going to be an effective change agent who reaches people, you must somehow study and seek to understand their problems. Only then should you begin developing solutions that meet their needs. The first part of solving any problem is understanding that problem in-depth. Then, once you think you have a sense of the root causes of the problem, you can begin thinking through how to formulate your solution to that problem.

As a leader with charisma and a clear vision, you will be able to speak to people with a conviction and with an authority that I believe they'll respond to. When I stand before many people who are obviously discouraged, one of my most important jobs is to help them see that there is a solution to their problems.

# DYNAMISM

If you want to cultivate healthy relationships with people, you would do well to develop dynamism. Now, what do I mean? Dynamism merely is your ability to be enthusiastic and passionate and personally involved in what you say and do. If I stood up in packed auditoriums of 1,000, 3,000, or 5,000 people, walked to the microphone, and started speaking in a very mellow, monotone way, they would probably tune me out immediately.

My friend, if I did that, I would be out of business. Fortunately, I'm passionate about the lives of people. I'm passionate about saving lives. It really does break my heart when someone commits suicide. It really bothers me that millions of people are depressed. It burdens me tremendously whenever I hear that a person has been molested or raped. I get upset every time I hear that a person has dropped out of high school.

Therefore, whenever I am scheduled to speak anywhere, I realize I may only have one chance to change a life. I might only have one opportunity to give someone hope. I might have only one chance to let someone know that they are here for a reason, and that life can get better.

Because so much is at stake, I cannot afford to go into speaking engagements and be calm and mellow. I must enter that speaking engagement with dynamism, regardless of what I might be going through in my own personal life. Irrespective of how I feel, I have to walk into those rooms and radiate that "Today is the day! Today is the day that your life can get better! Today is the day that you can turn things around! You can't go through life waiting for someone to turn your life around! You can do it for yourself! Now! Right now! Today!"

To have dynamism means you have to be physically and emotionally invested in what you're saying and doing.

Are you fired up about the stuff you talk about? Are you fired up because you care about people, and because you want to help them change their lives? Are you fired up because you want them to make the most of their lives? Are you fired up? Because if you're going to reach them, you need to be willing to talk with enthusiasm. You need to be willing to use gestures, or stand on chairs, or jump around, or spin in circles, or whatever else might work. Now, of course, that might not be a good idea if you are dealing with emotionally reserved, low-context students. I have made that mistake more than once, and I created tremendous distance with those audiences.

To be dynamic, you must be willing to step out of your comfort zone and do something that shows your heart. If you are dealing with emotionally demonstrative, high-context people, you've got to do something that they can feel. You have to do something that lets them know that you are passionate about what you are saying.

Yes, some might laugh. Maybe doing those kinds of things might make you uncomfortable. But again, if you want to reach them, please be willing to step out of your comfort zone. Try something that might be a little out of the box. By the way, what is "the box?" Who created it? I don't even like the box? Get excited!

Having said that, even if you're an introvert, there is a way for you to be invested in, and enthusiastic about, your work with people. There is a way for you to share your passion without having to holler. You do not have to scream, but you have to convey somehow you are fully invested in what you are saying.

For example, I recently watched Steven Spielberg's movie, Lincoln. That is one of the best movies I have seen in a long time. In the film, President Lincoln did not speak very loudly. He did not holler very often, but when he did talk, he spoke with passion. He spoke with dynamism. He spoke with a particular enthusiasm. He spoke with sincerity. He spoke with a certain authenticity that connected with me, and I believe connected with the nation. That man (or least Daniel Day Lewis's portrayal of him) touched people's lives without really raising his voice.

He didn't have a loud voice, and I do not have the strongest voice. However, I do have a deep commitment to helping people change their lives. I believe you have that same commitment. But don't be afraid to share your heart. To let your heart influence your demeanor and words. If it is real, do not be afraid to cry sometimes. Don't be afraid to raise your voice. Don't be afraid to do something that's drastic. Don't be afraid to do something that gets people's attention. Trust me, I am living proof that these things can help establish rapport with others. To be sure, I sometimes have gone too far in word or deed with some of my audiences. I have been in the moment and decided to take risks that did not have the effects I had intended. Even though things didn't go as planned, I have learned more from my failures than my successes. I have learned what not to do again, or I have learned how to do something more effectively. Your demonstrative attempts might not always go over very well, but keep trying them. You will learn about your own strengths and weaknesses, and discover some things that you might actually enjoy, and actually work.

# SERVING

The last step on the journey to real relationships is serving. The first nine attributes were leading to this point. The first nine characteristics were really preparing you to get to this point. Everything we do as teachers, speakers, or leaders is to serve the people with whom, and for whom, we work. When I say "serve," I am not referring to some kind of slave-like demeanor. Serving is the ability to connect to people in such a way that their dignity as human beings is affirmed and they are empowered to flourish.

Serving involves treating people with dignity and respect. Serving empowers people to write new, more fulfilling chapters in their lives. If you serve someone, you're affirming their worth as human beings in a way that helps them flourish or grow.

I once heard someone say, "You cannot serve someone that you do not really understand, and, if you try to serve someone you don't understand, you can become a benevolent oppressor." Wow! If you try to help someone that you do not know, then you can do more harm than good. To be sure, I am not saying you should not give homeless people your change, or that you should not help someone push their car if their car has stalled in the middle of an intersection. What I am saying is that if you want to help someone you see on a regular basis but have not taken the time to find out who they are or to understand their problems, then you could do more harm than good. Helping can sometimes hurt if it is not grounded in understanding.

Even though you have good intentions, your efforts could scar people emotionally. That kind of help can sometimes push people away. For example, as a child, I had so many people in my life who hurt me. They saw me as a project. They saw me as someone who needed to be fixed. They slapped all their solutions on me, but very few people ever took the time to find out who I was or the root causes of my problems.

I really just wanted to be loved. I wanted to be embraced. I wanted to be helped. I wanted someone to believe in me. I wanted to be accepted. Yes, my mother believed in me, but we had so many challenges at home that it was hard to notice her sometimes. As a kid, I just wanted someone to believe in me, someone to push me, someone to see my value, and someone to see my worth.

Those who ended up helping me the most were people who took the time to find out who I was and the problems I was facing. They took the time to meet me on my level and helped me. Those kinds of people change the world, one life at a time.

Friend, if you are going to reach anyone, you are going to have to start by building a healthy relationship with them. You're going to have to start by opening your heart and working on you. You are going to have to start by preparing yourself to address any issues in your own life and in your own background that could be in the way of you making a difference.

You have to address the lens through which you see the world so that you can position yourself to develop healthy relationships with others.

The road to healthy, life-giving relationships is paved with openness, acceptance, trust, learning, understanding, competence, commonality, charisma, dynamism and serving; and, I believe the primary purpose of building relationships with people is to serve them.

So the question becomes, "how can I best serve the people that I am trying to help?" The rest of the R.E.A.C.H. approach is my answer to that question.

## CHAPTER **FOURTEEN**

# ENGAGEMENT

One of the most important ways you can serve people is through engagement. In an earlier chapter, I told you that the first step in trying to reach a person is to build a relationship with them (after developing cultural self-awareness, of course). As important as it is to build relationships with people, sometimes relationships alone are not enough. If a student has terrible grades, it is not enough to just have a close-knit relationship with that person. That student needs to pick up his grades. That employee needs to improve her performance. Because of that, we cannot always relationship our way to success with people. Sometimes people need help making some significant changes in their lives. To help them, we must engage them.

What do I mean by engagement? Engagement involves capturing and keeping people's attention in unexpected, innovative, and positive ways. One of those ways is building culturally-relevant bridges between your audience's context and your content. Engagement at its best is about creating a bridge between context and content.

Earlier, I explained that, as a speaker, must **encode** your objectives by using **verbal**, **paraverbal**, **non-verbal**, and **non-action** to create a **message**. If you lack cultural self-awareness, all you have at your disposal to encode your objectives are your language and your personal experiences. Therefore, the words, sounds, and body language you use to encode your ideas reflect your own frame of reference. However, to be engaging, you must learn the language and dialect of your audience, and seek to understand their experiences. Only then can you use words, sounds, facial expressions, and body language to encode your objectives in a way that makes sense to your audience. Remember, even though you, as a speaker, determine the intentions of your message, it is your audience, ultimately, that determines the meaning of your messages. Your job as a communicator, teacher, or leader is to encode your objectives that make you engaging to your audiences. You must encode well to be engaging.

People don't learn or grow if they are bored, so as a teacher or speaker, you must engage them in unexpected, positive, innovative ways. Engage them in culturally responsive, developmentally appropriate ways, building a bridge between their contexts and your content, and from your content to their contexts, and from their context to your content, letting them see parts of their "normal" in your lesson or speech.

I think it's important here to make a distinction: trying to engage individuals is a little different from trying to engage an entire group of people. So for the rest of this chapter, I'll first share my thoughts on ways to engage individuals. Then, in the next section, I'll explain my views on how to engage groups. I have had a lot of experience walking into a room of strangers and trying to engage them on their levels.

With that said, what are some questions you can ask to engage individuals on their levels so that you can motivate them?

## WAYS TO ENGAGE INDIVIDUALS

There is a difference between the two types of people that you will be dealing with: someone with whom you already have a relationship, and someone that you do not know. If you're dealing with a person with whom you have some kind of history, then it's more appropriate for you to be able to walk into that person's life more informally and merely greet them with, "Hey {insert name}! How you doin?" If you sense something is wrong, you could ask, "is everything okay?" Or, you could even say, "Hey, you look like you have something on your mind. Is everything okay?" Or, "Hey, you seem like there's something going on. I see it in your eyes. If you ever want to talk, you know where to find me. I'm here for you."

The conversation can start off as simple as that. Sometimes those questions will open up an opportunity for you to really hear what's going on in a person's life. You see, it's easier for you to have those kinds of conversations with people with whom you already have a relationship with.

That leads me to my next point: you would do well to be the kind of person who is known as friendly. It would be nice if you had a reputation of being someone who cares about people. It would not hurt to become the "go-to" person- the person to whom people can go to whenever they have problems, or whenever they need someone to talk to. It would be helpful if you developed a reputation of being the kind of person who is warm and who exudes a welcoming attitude. Become the kind of person who greets people with love in your eyes. If you're that person, I guarantee you will have no shortage of people in your life seeking your advice, seeking your affirmation, or seeking to be in your presence. Simply because of the love that's flowing from your heart, you will become a magnet to whom people are drawn.

But let's say you are in a new situation, and you are around a new group of people who do not know you. What do you do then? Or let's say you're walking down the street and you see a young man sitting on a park bench. What in the world could you say or do to get his attention? This leads me into my discussion about the second kind of person that you will be dealing with.

Some people will come into your life that you do not know, and with whom you do not have any history. You have no idea about their past or their present. All you know is you want to add value to their lives somehow. That desire might be because you can sense that something is going on in that person's life.

You could ask that person a question. It could be a question related to something unique or interesting about them. When you engage a person, observe their body language, shoes, clothes—anything interesting to you that might allow you to start a conversation with that person. When you walk up to that person, you could just say something like "Man, those are some nice shoes you have on. What are they called?" "Man, you got a nice (hair)cut. Where can I go to get me a cut like that?" Or, you could ask something more indirect like, "Hey man, can you help me? I'm trying to find the nearest (insert whatever might need be nearby)?"

In any case, you want to start by expressing something that shows that you are sincerely interested in the individual as a person. You want to find a way to just ask a question that will get his or her attention. You can start asking questions that will help you assess this person's needs. But to do that, sometimes you can be very direct, whereas other times you need to be more subtle. In any case, your primary goal here is to assess the needs of the person that you are dealing with. You're trying to figure out what may be wrong.

You're trying to get a sense of who the person is. You want to understand what's going on at home. You want to get an understanding of what school he or she attends.

You want to then begin assessing what's something that might motivate the person. You need to think of a list of questions that will help you meet people right where they are. I also recommend you rehearse the questions you choose so that they come out naturally.

I recommend you start off on general, safe questions, then slowly ease into more personal questions. Also, I recommend you start with questions about the person's identity first, then ask questions about their goals and dreams and finally their obstacles. There is no formula. You have to find things that work for you. These are things that have worked for me.

Again, I think you should first ask general life questions, then dream questions, then obstacle questions. That way, the conversation progresses toward you being able to get a better sense of their perception about themselves and the world around them. Here are some questions you can use to begin thinking of your own questions.

## Questions to Start a Conversation:

- Where are you from? Were you born and raised here?

- How do you like the area?

- How did your family get to this area?

- What do you do for fun? Do you like riding your bike, playing video games, camping, wrestling, shopping?

- Do you have any pets? If so, what kind? What's his/her name?

- How did you get into _____? (Football, rapping, etc.)

- Do you like living in _____?

- Do you know your father? Do you have a relationship with him?

- Are you happy?

- Do you have a car?

- Do you have a job?

- Are you okay?

- You have any brothers or sisters?

- Are you on Facebook? Twitter? Instagram? Snapchat? Which one is the best?

- Have you ever been to a baseball game?

## Questions to Go Deeper

- Who do you live with?

- Where do you live? In what area?

- What is it like to live there?

- How is your relationship with your father and mother?

- What's going on at home?

- How are you doing in school? How are your grades?

- What grade are you in?

- What do you do when you're not in school?

- How long have you been in this area? This school? This state?

- How long have you _____? (Pick any topic that might be of interest to them.)

- How long have you and him/her been talking, or going together? (i.e., been in a relationship?)

- How many siblings do you have?

- Other than doing _____, what other sports, hobbies, etc, have you tried?

## Questions about Dreams and Goals:

- Do you want to be a professional athlete?

- You play sports?

- Do you want to go to college?

- You want to travel the world?

- You do want to own your own house?

- Do you want to drive a nice car?

- You want to make a lot of money?

- You want to be able to buy your mom a brand new house?

- What were your goals last year? Did you achieve them?

- In the past, did you achieve most of your goals?

- What are your plans for the future?

- What is your dream?

- What kind of house do you want to live in when you grow up?

- What is your vision for your life?

- What is your dream?

- Who do you want to be when you grow up?

- What are your personal goals for the year?

- How did you pick those as your top goals?

- Why did you pick those goals?

- What were your goals last year?

- What will it mean to you when your dream becomes your reality?

- What do you want to accomplish in the next year?

- What do you plan on doing in the next six months of your life?

- What's the most important goal for you to accomplish next year? How are you doing in terms of achieving your goals?

- Did you reach last year's goals?

- What were your New Year's resolutions?

- Have your goals been realistic in the past?

- How much money do you want to make?

- What would you do if you did not need money?

- If you could go anywhere in the world where would you go?

- How much traveling have you done in your life?

- Why do you want to travel?

- What kind of life do you want for your children?

- How are you going to pay for that kind of life?

- What school would you like to attend?

- What's your favorite college?

- Do you have any money saved up in your bank account?

- Do you have a bank account?

- Do you want children?

- How many children do you have?

- How many children do you want?

- Do you want a big home?

- Of all your goals, which is your most important goal this year? Which one do you want to achieve more than the others?

- What would you do if you did not need money?

- What do you plan on doing to achieve that goal?

- How do you determine whether you are getting closer to your goals?

- When do you plan on achieving your goal? Dream? What is your deadline?

- If you could go anywhere in the world, where would you go?

- Where do you want to go to college?

- How much money does it cost per year to go to that school?

- How much money do you have saved up for college?

- What kinds of things would you like to have in your dream home?

- How much money do you want to make every month? Every year?

- What kinds of things would you buy if you were financially free?

## Questions to Identify Obstacles

- What is preventing you from becoming what you want to be?

- Have you designed a plan to overcome your challenges?

- What must you overcome for your dreams to be realized?

- Why haven't you achieved your goals yet?

- What obstacle in your life is the most crucial to overcome?

- Are you making the progress necessary to overcome the obstacles that you have in your life?

- What are some things you can do to start overcoming some of these obstacles in your life?


Remember, your goal in asking these questions is to to get a sense of who this person is. You are not trying to be a psychologist; you're trying to be a friend.

It's at this point in the conversation that you are beginning to get a sense of who the person is, and where this person has been, where this person wants to go, the kind of person he or she wants to become; and, the kinds of obstacles that are keeping him or her from realizing those dreams. It's at this point that you can get a really good sense of his or her needs.

While he or she is answering your questions, you need to be thinking about what the person's highest hopes and needs are. Does he have father issues? Has her father been gone his whole life? Does he even know who his father is? Is her attitude helping or hurting her? If so, try to get at the root of why he or she has a bad mood?

I can't stress enough that you're going to need the patience to get a person's attention. Is the person homeless? Does she have an unstable home life? Has he moved from place to place to place, year after year, and has no real roots in any one community? Does this person have a drug problem? Does he smoke marijuana? Does she sell drugs? Does her neighborhood have gangs? What are the names of the gangs in that person's neighborhood? Does he wear clothes or have tattoos that might indicate he's involved in gang activity?

Can she form a sentence correctly? Is he always tired? Does this person seem like he needs to see a counselor? Is this person suicidal? Is she depressed? Does the person have low self-esteem? Is the person need to know what it feels like to be loved unconditionally? Is this person having sex with several people to find some kind of love or affirmation? Does this person wear a lot of makeup because she doesn't feel attractive? Does this person have a hard time making eye contact with you?

Does the person hang out in your classroom long after school gets out? That might be an indication that this person doesn't want to go home, which might tell you that there are some problems at home? This would be an excellent opportunity for you to ask questions about that. All of these issues mentioned above give you a good sense of the kinds of things that this person is going through.

What's important here is that you assess where this person is by engaging them with relevant, genuine questions. You don't want to conduct an interview, you want to have an inner-view in which you get an inner, intimate look into the life of this person.

In my case, I dropped out of high school and was sitting on a park bench. A man named Martin walked up to me and engaged me with a question. He asked, "Hey man, what are you doing out here on the school day?" He expected an answer, but he didn't have a judgmental tone. He seemed like he was genuinely curious. He seemed like a big brother asking a younger brother a question. Also, his demeanor- concerned, patient, calm- made him look like someone I could trust.

So I answered his question. He was trying to establish a common ground with me. That question was enough to get my attention. He seemed like he just wanted to have a conversation. He started sharing a little bit about himself, and he let me know that he understood my pain. He asked me questions like, "man, where's your father?" I told him my father was locked up. He asked me where my mom was; I said to him that mom was at home and mom was struggling. His questions gave him a sense of who I was, and some of the things I was going through.

From my responses to his questions, Martin could discern that I did not have a place where I felt loved. Martin could sense that I may have had father issues because my father had been gone for all of my life. He recognized that I was not truly happy. He probably noticed I was tired too. I'm pretty sure that while we were talking, he was thinking about ways to help me.

I need to repeat this: you are there to come off as a friend who genuinely cares about the person, not as some guru or superhero. You're there to be a listening ear. You're there to show that you support the person. You're there to be that person's advocate. You're on his team. You want the best for her.

During your conversation, it would not hurt you to simply pause and just spend time being very present with them. Just sit there with them and let them know, through your body language, voice, and facial expressions, that you care about them. Only when you are listening can you really begin to find out what a person needs.

Engaging an individual takes intentionality. With people becoming more private and guarded, establishing rapport with them is going to require you to work harder than you are used to working. From my experience, however, everyone wants a friend who will listen to them. Why not start working to become that kind of friend for more people in your life?

CHAPTER **FIFTEEN**

# ENGAGING A GROUP

In this chapter, I'd like to share my thoughts about engaging an entire group. There are vast differences between engaging an individual and a group. Each situation has its own challenges. Maybe you are a teacher, or a small group leader, or someone who leads a group or an organization or a team, and you would like to know what you can do to reach a group. To engage anyone, especially a group, you have to be creative. You just have to do some things that will require you to have a little courage.

In the last chapter, I mentioned that engagement involves capturing and keeping people's attention in unexpected, innovative, positive ways by building culturally-relevant bridges between your audience's contexts and your content. It is about letting people see parts of their "normal" in your lessons or speech. How exactly can you do that with a group? How do you actually use your understanding of others in your lesson plans and interactions with them so that they can see themselves in your curriculum?

Let me show you how engagement looks with groups. I'll never forget the day my English teacher, who grew up in a gated community in an affluent neighborhood, walked into my class of blacks, Latinos, Asians, and several poor white students. She handed out syllabi with names on it like Shakespeare, Chaucer, Hemingway, and Frost. My friend folded it into a paper airplane and threw it at her. He asked, "Why you got us reading about a bunch of dead white guys who wore tights?" He was saying, indirectly, "There is nothing on this syllabus that any of us can relate to. We feel like we live in an undeclared war zone, and nothing on your syllabus is going to help any of us survive what we live through every day. As my colleague, Baruti Kafele, says, in essence, "there is nothing here that allows me to see myself in your curriculum. I don't see myself."

Please do not miss this: you teach what's relevant, important, what's significant, and what matters by what you say, do, and include in your curriculum or business plans. You also teach what's not important, what's not relevant, what doesn't matter by what you don't say and don't do, and who you don't include in your syllabi or in your plans. Who might you be leaving out of your curriculum? Who might you be leaving out of your business? Can the people you want to reach see themselves in your curriculum or presentation? Can they see the beautiful tapestry, the mosaic of the country and world in which we live? If they cannot see themselves in your curriculum or presentations, you may be unintentionally and unknowingly telling them, "you and people like you don't matter to me." If your students or audience cannot see themselves in your lessons or presentations, then you become one of the biggest barriers that keep them from learning and growing. By choosing not to let your students or audience see their "normal" in your presentation, you become the person that pushes them away. You become the reason they're not engaged. You become the reason they drop out of school. You become the reason they keep their heads down. You become the reason they become apathetic.

I'll never forget the day I saw myself for the first time in a teacher's curriculum. My English teacher had this idea that she wanted to teach about some rhetorical tropes and figures. She wanted to teach us about antithesis, but she knew she couldn't start by examining the works of Shakespeare. She knew she couldn't use Chaucer, Hemingway, or Frost. She had to use somebody with whom we were familiar.

She walked into class and said to us, "You guys, I wanna tell you about what Two-pack Shaker said." She mispronounced his name, but we were pleasantly surprised by her effort. She continued, he said, "I'd rather die like a man than live like a coward; there's a ghetto up in heaven, and it's ours. Black power!" We were in shock and joyous awe! A teacher included one of our heroes in her lesson plan!

Don't make the mistake of thinking that I am telling you to use rap in your curriculum. I am not. What I am telling is that it's not about rap, but about becoming a student of your students and meeting them on their levels. It's about becoming a student of your audiences so that you can include things from their cultural universe in your lessons or speeches. It's about becoming a student of your students, humbling yourself, de-centering yourself, and seeking to enter into the world of those you want to reach as a humble servant-leader. Engagement is about trying to understand patterns of thinking, feeling and behaving, language, symbols, heroes, rituals, worldviews, values, and then seeking to incorporate some of those things, when relevant, into your curriculum or presentations.

I've used that same principle in my own work for the last 18 years. When I go to the hood, I start where the students are. I ask them to teach me about who they are and what they like. I ask them if they are fans of Cardi B, Future, 21 Savage, Migos, Quavo, Jigga, Kendrick Lamar or whoever is popular in the media at the moment. When they hear their heroes included in my "curriculum," they lean in with excitement. After I have them hooked, I then go more in-depth and connect their contexts with my content, whatever it might be for that particular audience.

If I visit a predominantly white area, I decenter myself as much as I can and start where my audience is. I ask them to teach me a little bit about them. Do they like Slipknot, ACDC, Maroon 5, Cary Underwood, Tim McGraw, Sponge Bob, Instagram, Snapchat or whoever or whatever else I think they might like or dislike. They usually lean in, sitting at the edge of their seats, ready to learn whatever I want to teach them. I connect their context with my content.

Furthermore, if I speak in a predominantly Latino, Spanish-speaking area, I decenter myself and try to start where my audience is. I practice some of my Spanish with them and ask them to teach me about who they are and what they like. They lean in, at the edge of their seats, and eagerly listen to whatever I want to teach them. Again, I connect their context to my content.

Friends, the key to engaging an individual or a group is building culturally-relevant bridges between your audience's context with your content; and, build another bridge between your content and their contexts. You repeat that bridge-building process over and over again. When you do that, something powerful happens! People lean in, they smile, they sit up straight, and they hang onto your every word. Why? You have engaged them.

Teacher, your students at the bottom of your class can learn. So don't dumb down your lessons. Don't feel sorry for them or coddle them into mediocrity. Don't pity them if they live in poverty. They can learn. They are smart. Although they might not know how to make their subjects and verbs agree, many of them have PhDs in urban existentialism with an emphasis in ghetto eschatology. They have a knowledge of a different kind. Don't lower your standards, but build bridges between their context and your content, between your content and their contexts, and watch the magic of learning take place.

Study, study, study your audience! Study your students! Then, incorporate your new understandings into your curriculum, into your lesson plans, or into your speeches. Build bridges related age, sex, race and ethnicity, gender, psychological make-up, beauty, communication styles, politics, social structure and class, individualism-collectivism, uncertainty avoidance, power distance, and any other cultural variable that you think could help engage your students or audiences. If you do that, more heads will come off the desks, more earphones will come out of their ears, and more light bulbs will come on in their eyes. When you are engaging, the magic of learning takes place.

Here are some more examples of ways you can be engaging.

# MUSIC

Right off the bat, you can always use music to get a group's attention. You can watch a video, listen to a song, sing a song, rap, or play the song yourself. If you can sing or play an instrument, or rap, you can use those talents to engage your audiences. They will perk up, laugh, and get with you.

If you are not comfortable with your singing voice, you can still recite the lyrics to one of your favorite songs, and unpack the meaning for the group. Or, you can have them try to explain the meaning of the song to you.

Or, you can watch MTV, or BET, or google the top 100 songs in the country to find out what kind of music people are listening to. You can also ask them directly: who are you guys listening to? Who is your favorite rapper, singer, performer? Who is your favorite group? What is your favorite song? They will tell you what they like, and you can use that as a starting point.

# TELEVISION and MOVIES

You can use scenes from shows and movies to introduce or illustrate a point you want to make. You can use those things to open your lesson plan. You can use those things to engage people. Find out what is popular on television, and use it as a starting point for your lesson plan. Or, you could use it to illustrate one of your points.

# ENVIRONMENT

You could set up your room differently. You can arrange the chairs in a circle, or put them against the wall and have everyone sit on the floor.

Or you could put posters and pictures on the walls that are interesting or unique or poignant.

If you are outside, you could start a campfire or something that is exciting and different.

# ROLE PLAY

If you are discussing an issue have each participant tell a story that is relevant to the topic, relevant to the subject or theme or issue. Role-playing involves having each participant tell a different part of the story, sharing a different perspective.

# BEHAVIOR MODELING

You could also do behavior modeling by having your group practice a skill using a four-step method: You do it for them; you do it with them; they do it alone while you observe them; you give them feedback about what you observed.

# CASE STUDIES

Have participants tell them about a problem, (written or verbally), then ask them to identify the issues, analyze that situation, brainstorm some possible solutions to the problem, and then propose what they recommend be done to address the problem.

You can do case studies on a drive-by shooting or about a controversial policy. In fact, you can talk about anything you want. You can present it in a way that forces them to address the problem personally. You can say something like, "If someone walked into your, living room and they had this problem (name problem), and this is their background, and these are resources you have to work with (tell them about their resources), what would you recommend for this person? What would you recommend be done to help that person. These are just few examples of case studies. Use them or make up your own.

# DEBATE

You can use debates in your classroom or with your group. Pick a Resolution like, "Students should be required to wear uniforms in school." Then form two teams (2 people on each team). One group argues in support of the Resolution. The second group argues against it. They take turns presenting their arguments, while the rest of the class takes notes and prepares questions to ask at the end of the debate.

For Resolutions, you can pick any topic. You can pick the same topics from the presidential elections; you can pick a topic you know about; you can talk about cloning; you could talk about music, you can talk about style, about language, politics, or whatever is a hot topic.

Give them time to prepare for the debate. Then, on the day of your debate, set up your classroom like it is a debate hall. Introduce the Resolution, then each team (they can have a group name), and then get the debate underway: "I'd like to call upon the first speaker of the affirmative (speaker's name) to open the debate." Someone argues the affirmative case. Someone argues the negative. Then you call for the 2nd Affirmative, then the 2nd Negative. Then the 3rd Affirmative and 3rd Negative.

Let your group observe and let the two teams go at it. You would be surprised and impressed at the things that your group come up with, and you'll probably get no shortage of laughs from some of the things that they come up with. It is a beautiful thing when you see people sharing their ideas creatively and with passion. If you work with students, you might even discover a future lawyer or politician or leader.

## DIALOGUE

Have two people hold a conversation while the other participants observe, and ask questions. Let two people talk in front of the class about an issue and then let others discuss it and ask questions. The entire class can inform the conversation or just move the conversation along. Ask speakers for clarification, ask them to go deeper, ask them what they mean, and to defend their point(s). Ask questions that might challenge their position, or just allow the discussion to take place. Use the Socratic Method: ask questions of everyone in your class and make sure everyone participates. If someone asks a question and the person doesn't know the answer to the question, let the class chime in, or maybe you can chime in, or you can give them a little hint.

## DRILLS

Use some drills where your group repetitively practices a skill. Maybe it is some task that you want them to do, maybe it's passing out papers at the beginning of the class. You might want to help them learn to do that effectively because doing that well can save you hours of instruction time. It can give you more time to focus on lesson plans and spend less time passing out paperwork and handouts. Practice a skill. Have them go through it at the beginning of the class, or even on the first day of class.

## FIELD TRIPS

Allow people to experience the world outside of school or the office. Expose them to more. I believe exposure is the birthplace of big dreams and motivation. Take them to a location to observe tasks being performed. The trip can be carefully planned with regard to learning objectives so that it is both fun and educational. My teacher took us on a few field trips. We once went to the Museum of Tolerance in Los Angeles, and that museum had no small impact on me and my classmates.

## PREPARING YOURSELF TO BE YOUR BEST

I need to say something else about engagement. You cannot just roll out of bed and be engaging. If you just wake up, clean the sleep out of your eyes, and walk into your class or your presentation, you have already placed yourself at a considerable disadvantage.

To be engaging, you have to get yourself ready before you stand before any group of people. You get yourself ready by preparing your mind, your emotions, your body, and your voice. I lay out a process to get yourself "salty" in my other book, *Even on Your Worst Day You Can Be a Student's Best Hope.* Here I will just say that you need to get yourself ready to be your best every single day you plan to stand before a group of people to teach or speak.

You must make the content that you're about to talk about exciting for yourself. When you look at your curriculum, do you still get excited about it? When you think about your presentation, do you still get excited about it? If you don't, why would other people be excited about it? If you're not engaging, why would other people be engaged? If you're not excited about what you're talking about, why would others care about it? If you are not passionate about the work that you do, how can you inspire passion in other people? If you're not walking every day with purpose, how can you help other people find theirs? You cannot just roll out of bed and be engaging.

After a full day of work, when you are looking at yourself in the mirror, can you honestly say that you have done your best? I heard Gardner Taylor tell the story of a man who was on a cruise ship. I believe the man's name was Edwin. The ship Edwin was on hit something and started to sink. In a panic, Edwin jumped overboard and swam to shore. Once he reached the shore, he looked back out at the water, and he saw a bunch of people struggling, and nearly drowning. So Edwin swam back out, grabbed one, and swam that person to shore. Edwin looks back out and sees more people struggling. He swam back out and rescued another one. Edwin went out and back over 18 times and rescued several more people.

When he had no more strength left, he collapsed on the sand in exhaustion. While laying there, he looked out at the water and saw people's heads go underwater never to emerge again at the surface. They had drowned.

That night, when Edwin was in his hospital bathroom, he stared himself in the mirror. He said, "Edwin, did you do your best? Could you have saved one more? Did you do your best?"

My question to you, are you doing your best? If you are not doing your best, you could lose someone. To prevent the loss of any more people, do your best by waking up early, and prepare your mind, your heart, your body, your soul to help people by being engaging.

# CHAPTER **SIXTEEN**

# AWARENESS

The "A" in R.E.A.C.H. stands for awareness. It's not enough to build a relationship with people you want to reach, although relationships are fundamental. It's not enough to engage people on their levels so they can see themselves in your curriculum or presentations, although cultural relevance is vital. What's as important than those two things is helping the people you want to reach to become painfully AWARE of the imbalances in their lives.

Underperforming people do not change because we want them to change. Ultimately, people change when they become painfully aware of some imbalance in their lives (physically, mentally, relationally, financially, spiritually, professionally, educationally, etc.). That is called disequilibration.

I believe everyone is motivated by two things: their desire to avoid pain and their desire to gain pleasure. I believe people are motivated by pain and pleasure. I believe when people are in pain they are disequilibrated.

Everything we do is motivated by the pain or the pleasure we link to it mentally. Think about it. Think of everything you have done in your life, good and bad. I bet most of your actions and decisions have been deeply rooted in either your desire to gain pleasure or your desire to avoid pain. Why do you go to work every day? Why do you go shopping at Christmas? Why do you wear make-up? Why are you in the relationship that you are in? Why do you hang out with that group? You want to avoid pain or experience pleasure, that's why.

Why do most people fail to lose the weight they want to lose? They would rather experience the pleasure of enjoying a meal than the pain of exercising. Why don't most people follow through on the goals that they set? They believe the pain they will experience from trying to change will be too high. Why don't most people keep their New Year's resolutions they make on December 31st? Or why don't people follow through on commitments that they make? I think it is because of one or two reasons. They want to experience pleasure or avoid pain.

When it comes to change, people are the same way. Therefore, we need to help them link pain and pleasure to the behaviors and the attitudes and the actions for the people you want to reach. People need to feel the pain that comes from being unbalanced in some area of their lives.

Why is becoming painfully aware of one's own imbalances so important? I believe that most people don't change because they feel like it. They don't change because they think it's a good idea. Rather, most people change because they must. They change because they believe they must.

Until people get to a place where they realize they have to change, they will not change. I'm convinced that to change, you must get to a place where you're sick and tired of feeling sick and tired.

A man was walking by a junkyard, and he saw a dog sitting outside of the junkyard, howling. It's obvious the dog was in pain. So the man walks into the junkyard office, and said, "there's a dog outside, and he's howling. Is he your dog?"

"Yeah, yeah...he's mine. He's sitting on a nail, " the owner replied.

Confused, the good samaritan asked, "then why doesn't he get up, off of the nail?"

To that, the owner said, "Oh he will, when it hurts bad enough."

In the same way, some of the people you want to reach are sitting on a figurative nail. They might be complaining about the nail, and crying about the nail. But they will never get up off of the nail until it hurts them bad enough. Therefore, our job is simply to help people we want to reach become more painfully aware of the nails in their lives.

How can you use pain and pleasure in your lesson plans or presentations? How can use pain and pleasure in your one-on-one meetings? How can you get leverage in those situations? I believe questions are the answer. I want to share three questions with you that have helped me get leverage over my own life and enabled me to help other people get leverage over their own lives.

Three questions: what have you missed out on because of your behavior, that belief, or your attitude? What are you missing out on because of your behavior, belief, or attitude? What will you miss out on because of this behavior, belief, or attitude?

I bet you their responses are quite revealing. Maybe they have missed out on getting good grades or having healthy relationships. Perhaps they are missing out on opportunities to play a sport or travel. Maybe they will not be able to go to college, get a good job, buy a beautiful house, or help people. The answers people give are always compelling.

If you want to help anyone change, it is vital for you to help them become keenly aware of the imbalances in their lives. It is crucial for you to help them get leverage over their situations by linking pain to the harmful beliefs and behaviors and pleasure to the ethical beliefs and behaviors. If you want to help them to succeed, you have to help them link pain to procrastination, and link pleasure to the hard work. You have to help them link pain to missing school, and link pleasure to your classroom or location. You have to help them link pain to watching too much television, and pleasure to reading a good book. You have to help them understand that the pain of discipline is much better than the pain of regret.

You have to help them link pain to talking back in class, or being disrespectful; and link pleasure to showing up early, being fully present in class, and doing homework as soon as they get out of school. You must help them link pleasure to it.

So, begin thinking how can you use pain and pleasure in your lesson plans or presentations. How can you use pain and pleasure to help people feel the imbalances in their lives? Here are some more questions you could ask people to help them become painfully aware of the imbalances in their lives.

# MORE QUESTIONS

- What is preventing you from being where you want to be?

- What is in the way of you picking up your grades?

- What is in the way of you graduating from high school?

- What are some of the issues you have to deal with that are limiting your potential?

- Have you designed a plan to overcome the obstacles you are facing?

- What are you doing to overcome _____(specific obstacle)?

- What are you doing to overcome your bad grades?

- Which issues are you facing that have been the most difficult to overcome?

- What are some things you have tried to overcome these obstacles/challenges?

- What have you done to address these challenges? Have any of them worked?

Questions like these will help put you in the position to give people the solutions they need to turn their lives around.

# TELL THE TRUTH

Only after you have asked questions, and earned the right to ask hard questions, can you then point out, or at least suggest some imbalances that are in people's lives. Having said that, sometimes you need to flat out tell the truth as you see it lovingly. Make sure that what your conclusions are not stronger than your evidence before you say things to people, or else you could lose credibility with them.

Let me give you an example of how telling the truth can help one become aware of his or her imbalances. I weighed 165 pounds when I graduated from high school. In college, I played a little football for a couple years and got up to 185 pounds of mostly muscle. When I stopped playing football, I got up to about 195 pounds. Then, when I got married and started enjoying my wife's cooking, I got up to 200 pounds. Then, over the last ten years, I somehow gained a lot more weight.

For years, I jogged occasionally, but not regularly. I ate whatever I wanted, and gained a little weight. But, I never thought it was a problem. I thought I still looked good, that I was still strong and healthy. After all, I played college football!

Well, a little while ago, I went to my doctor for a physical. Knowing that they were going to weigh me, I wore my lightest clothes. I was hoping that I could take off a few pounds just by the clothes I was wearing. I weighed a whopping 235 pounds! I'm not tall enough to weigh that much, but, to be honest, I really didn't think it was a problem.

The nurses also took my blood pressure and checked my blood.

When my doctor walked into the room, we talked for a little bit about life, and about our families. Then he looked at his clipboard with my information on it, and then looked up at me, and shot straight with me—he said, "you are obese!"

I laughed; he didn't.

He said again, "you are obese! You're not even an American."

Then I really laughed. He didn't. I said, "Doc I was born in Denver, Colorado."

He replied, "No! You're not even an American! Your body mass index is 33. Americans have a body mass index of 31. So, if you get down to 31, I can then welcome you to America. And THAT'S not a compliment my friend, because Americans are obese! You're obese!"

I just stared at him.

It got even more delightful. "You have high blood pressure, high cholesterol, and you're a black male—so you have a higher risk of getting prostate cancer. You have a family, a wife, three beautiful kids. You are traveling the world helping others, and I'm concerned that things are not looking good for your future. You might not live very well, or very long. And I'm trying to be nice."

How do you think I felt when my doctor hit me with that haymaker of truth? Quite imbalanced. I became painfully aware of what was at stake. I began to think about my family, and my wife, and my kids, and my work, and my mission. I didn't have a father, and never want my kids to experience the pain of growing up without a dad. Also, I didn't think it was fair for my wife to have to raise my kids on her own, because I was sick, or dead. I thought about not being able to see my kids grow up, graduate from high school; go to college, and graduate; to get married—I thought about not being able to walk my daughter down the aisle at her wedding; I thought about missing out on life because of my poor health, and lack of self-control, and lack of discipline. I was obese, and I was very aware of it.

In that state of awareness about my obesity, my doctor asked me a question, "if you don't get ahold of yourself, what do you think is going to happen to you? You probably don't want that, do you?"

He had me right where he wanted me—painfully aware of the imbalances in my life.

I sat in that doctor's office feeling very uncomfortable about myself and my weight. I was a little embarrassed to be talked to in that way. I was obese. "Manny Man," Mr. Popular, the one who all the ladies loved in college … is obese! "What in the world has happened to me? How did I get this out of control?" I thought.

Helping people become aware of their imbalances is probably the most critical part of reaching anyone. This chapter alone is probably worth the price of the entire book because it lays out why people do what they do, and why they change. In that doctor's office, with such hard truth, I no longer just wanted to get in shape, I had to get in shape. I no longer just felt like losing weight was a good idea; it became an inescapable must.

When you have someone in that position, painfully aware of their imbalances, you don't have much more work to do to reach them.

Let me tell you another story about a young man I used to mentor. He was a gang member whose father died in his arms from gang violence. He was going down that same path as his father. To try to help him, I spent months trying to build a relationship with him. After I had earned his trust, I took him to a cemetery and had a heart to heart conversation with him. We talked about tombstones. I told him, "you can't control your birth date or your death date. All you have control over is that dash in between your birth date and death date. Are you happy with what you've done with your dash? What have you missed out on, what are you missing out on, what will you miss out on because of your choices—because of what you are doing with your dash? Are you happy with what you've done with your dash?" He hollered at me, "Naw, I ain't happy!" I then asked him, "Where are you going to be in one year if you keep going down this path?" He replied, "I'm going to be dead."

Later that night he said to me, "I wanna go back to school. These streets ain't for me. Can you help me?" He got his GED, he enrolled in college and got a full scholarship. He is now a music producer.

My point is this: I earned the right to ask that young man lovingly intrusive questions, and helped him become aware of the imbalances in his life.

Friend, when you help to disequilibrate someone, they are in the perfect position to hear about solutions that can help them restore their equilibrium. They are in the perfect position to persuaded to make changes in their lives.

# CHAPTER **SEVENTEEN**

# CONVINCE

You serve people by engaging them and helping them become aware of the imbalances in their lives. When people feel an imbalance in their lives—their equilibrium has been disturbed—they are inclined to change. They are open to anything that will help them restore their equilibrium. That is where "C" in R.E.A.C.H. comes in. "C" stands for convince. We have to convince people that they can succeed in school, work, or life. We have to convince them that education is the key to their problems. We have to convince them that a good education can restore their equilibrium. We have to convince them education can help give them back their balance. We need to convince people that working hard has its rewards. We need to help them see that what we are recommending to them meets their needs.

When you help people become painfully aware of some of the imbalances in their lives, you are in the position to make some recommendations to them. You are now able to serve as an advisor who pitches some things to them that might help them alleviate their pain. This is where you have to convince them.

We must convince them that school is a better way. We must convince them that it is vital for them to do their homework. We must convince people to take your advice.

How do you convince someone of anything? I believe you should lead with their needs. In other words, we need to lead our recommendation to them with their needs in mind. Whatever their need is, you need to think of how school, or church, or whatever, benefits them.

You need to talk about how your recommended solution helps them. It is all about them. What's in it for them? What will they get out of it? How will it empower them? How will it equip them? How will it make them feel? How will it help their bank balances?

You have to sell your solution to them. You have to sell pleasure to them. You have to sell enjoyment to them. Whether you like it or not, you are in the sales business—we all are. We have to sell ideas every day, in our homes, to our spouses, to our relatives, to our kids, and to others. To convince anyone of anything, we need not talk about why we like something. Instead, we should talk about why or how it benefits them.

So let me ask you, what is it that you do for a living? What are you selling? Are you selling education? Are you selling a product? Are you selling a service? What are you selling? Next, what are the benefits of what you sell? Why would someone buy it from you? Write down exactly what it is you are trying to sell to the person you want to reach.

If you are an educator, you are not selling school; you are selling opportunity. You are not selling homework; you are selling success. You are not selling an essay; you are selling the power to communicate clearly. You are not reading; you are selling critical thinking skills, which lead to success. You get the idea. Think about what you are selling, and the benefits of it.

For example, if someone wants to play sports, you can say, "Hey, if you do your homework you'll be able to pick up your grades. If you pick up your grades, you'll be eligible to play sports. If you are eligible to play sports, you might be able to get a scholarship. Furthermore, if you get a scholarship to go to college, you might be able to get drafted to play professional sports. However, even if you don't go pro, you can still graduate from college and get a nice job, start a business, make a living and a difference in the world." That is all about benefits.

I've found that you don't need to talk about the cost of what you're talking about, because if you give someone a big enough "Why?" they are not as concerned about the "how much?" Their desire to experience the pleasure of the benefits will more than likely motivate them to do whatever is necessary to attain those benefits.

When you are trying to convince people to do anything, you may also need to point out the pain in their lives. For some reason, people do more out of fear of loss than they do to gain some pleasure. From my experience, people work harder if they are afraid they are going to lose their jobs than they will to get a promotion.

In any case, you need to share with them your solutions. Share with them your recommendations. Tell them, "you need to come to this group, you need to come to class, you need to show up early," or something like that. No matter what you say, talk about the benefits of what you are asking them to do.

For example, if a student is always running late, talk about the benefits of showing up early, or the consequences of showing up late. Talk about the benefits of getting enough sleep at night or the consequences of being too tired. Talk about the benefits of getting up early to prepare their hearts, minds, and bodies for a day of productive work; or about the pain of regret for not being prepared. Talk about the benefits of paying attention when they are in class. Talk about the benefits of being fully attentive to what their teachers and what others are saying, or the consequences of not paying attention. Talk about the benefits of doing homework before they hang out with friends or the consequences of not turning in their homework. Talk about the benefits of reading books, of reading magazines, of writing, and the consequences of not being able to express themselves clearly.

If you teach math, talk about the benefits of learning equations. Whatever it is you are selling, talk about the benefits of learning whatever it is that you want them to learn. Talk about the benefits of asking for help. Talk about the benefits of being able to just admit that you need help. Talk about the benefits of exercising. Talk about the benefits. I'm repeating a lot because repetition is the mother of learning. I want you to get this. If you get this, you'll reach more people, save more lives, make a big difference, perhaps make more money, and create a lasting legacy. You see, those are the real benefits of you reading this book. It is not about me. This book is about what you can achieve as a result of reading this book.

## References and Self-Concept

Ultimately, the quality of our lives is based on our habits. That is, the things we do daily ultimately determines the quality of our lives. Furthermore, our habits are based on our actions; our actions are based on our decisions; our decisions are based on our emotions; and, our emotions are based on our beliefs.

So if you want to help people change their lives, you must change their beliefs. What are beliefs? Beliefs are feelings of certainty about something. Beliefs are feelings that something is true. They are feelings that something corresponds to reality. How do you change someone's beliefs to change their lives?

To answer that question, we need to discuss references, because beliefs- feelings of certainty- are based on references. Why do we believe what we believe? Because we have references for those beliefs. References are the foundation upon which our beliefs are built. References are experiences we've had, ideas we've learned, people we've met, dreams we've had. The more references someone has for a belief, the stronger that person's emotional attachment to that belief.

For example, I used to believe that I was not college material. I used to believe that people like me—with my background—could not go to college. From where did I get that belief? Everyone in my family dropped out of school. Because of those references, I somehow came to believe that people like me don't go to college. Those were my references. However, I had a teacher take my friends and me to a college campus and helped us see that we too could attend college. She had us eat lunch with college students. While the students were talking, I sat there quietly because I was intimidated. I didn't believe I was smart enough to be at the table with them. I didn't think I belonged there. There was no one there who looked like me.

However, one of the college students started talking, and he didn't sound that smart. I remember sitting up, staring at him, and saying to myself, "If he's in college, and he doesn't sound that smart, then maybe I can go to college too!" That one reference changed my belief about myself being able to go to college.

Furthermore, I used to think that all white people were rich, and would try to hurt my loved ones and me. But I had a white teacher who drove a convertible rabbit, and who only had $20 in her bank account. She helped me apply to college, and I couldn't understand why a white woman seemed to care so much about my future. She was white, and she was not rich, and she did not try to hurt me. That one reference—my white teacher—changed my belief about white people.

I have thousands of references like that that have changed my life. I bet you have thousands of references too that have changed your beliefs, and ultimately your life.

I share the importance of references with you because some of the people you want to reach might have some self-sabotaging beliefs that need to be addressed; and, I share that primarily because you might be the only reference they will ever have to change that self-sabotaging belief.

Exposure is the birthplace of motivation and big dreams. Expose your students to more than rapping, rebounding, robbing, and other limiting models. Give people glimpses of their own possibilities. Let them meet people who have overcome challenges similar to their own. Let your students read about them, watch them on TV, or even meet them in person. Expose the people you want to reach to more than their normal.

By doing so, you help them see themselves succeeding. By exposing them to people with whom they can identify, you help them catch glimpses of their own possibilities. You give them the chance to see themselves excelling. If people can see themselves succeeding in their heads, and believe those visions in their hearts, they can achieve their visions in their lives.

So convince them that they are more significant than their circumstances. Convince them that just because they live in the hood, that the hood doesn't have to live in them. Convince them by giving them references that inspire them to imagine themselves succeeding in school, work, or life.

Help them see that they can become the first person in their families to graduate from high school; that they can have a thriving trade; that they can graduate from college if they want; and, that they can build meaningful lives for themselves.

If you convince them with inspiring references, they will start to believe in themselves, and start to feel better emotionally, and will be in the perfect position to make the decisions they need to make, and take the actions they need to take, develop healthy habits; and, ultimately, achieve their dreams.

# CHAPTER **EIGHTEEN**

# **HAND**

How do you serve the people you want to reach? You engage them in positive, innovative, unexpected ways by building culturally relevant bridges into their lives. You then help them become painfully aware of the imbalances in their lives physically, mentally, emotionally, educationally, vocationally, professionally, financially, relationally, or spiritually. Next, you must convince them they can succeed in school, work, or life by giving them references that will change their beliefs, their emotions, their decisions, their actions, their habits, and, ultimately, the quality of their lives. Finally, you must reach out your hand to them.

The "H" in R.E.A.C.H. stands for Hand. If you want to serve someone, you must reach out your hand, figuratively, and quite often, literally. Let me explain.

When I was in such a bad place in my life, sitting on that park bench, you would not have been able to convince me that I could get straight As in school. You would not have been able to convince me that I could graduate from high school, go to college, be happily married, become a loving father, own a home, fly airplanes, or become the person I am today. I was in such a bad place that I could not imagine myself succeeding in school, work, or life. I honestly did not see myself making past my 18th birthday.

So I needed someone to build a relationship with me. Initially, I needed someone to engage me, help me become painfully aware of my need to change my life, I needed someone to give me a glimpse of my own possibilities, and, most importantly, I needed someone to reach out his or her hand to walk with me.

I needed someone to walk me through Vygotsky's (1978) Zone of Proximal Development (ZPD) helping me reach the next step that I was capable of achieving. The ZPD is the area between the child's current developmental level "as determined by independent problem solving" and the level of development that the child could achieve "through adult guidance or in collaboration with more capable peers (86). That guidance is called scaffolding. Based on Vygotsky's theory, I am entirely convinced that I needed people to provide scaffolding for me in my ZPD. I needed people to cultivate a relationship with me so they could identify my ZPD. That is, I needed people to meet me on my cognitive level and walk with me as a mentor, a friend, and a guide.

Fortunately, that is what happened to me. Teachers, administrators, coaches, food service workers, custodians, bus drivers, nurses, librarians, security guards, secretaries, and others provided the scaffolding for me to learn, grow, and succeed in school. They also laid the foundation for me to continue excelling in college, work, and in life.

I had people walking with me, figuratively. Their examples encouraged and inspired me to do my best. Their thoughtful advice challenged me to break some bad habits. They became the references I needed to cut some of the self-sabotaging beliefs that I had.

One of the most important things I have learned about success is that it is your habits, not your hardships, that ultimately position you for happiness. Because of that, people must learn to develop healthy habits that will position them to succeed in school, work, and life.

However, as I have explained, habits are built upon actions, actions are built upon decisions, decisions are built upon emotions, and emotions are based on beliefs.

At the end of the day, if you want your life to get better, you must have beliefs that put you in a good emotional space to make sound decisions, that lead to you taking action, and, ultimately, developing healthy habits.

Therefore, if you want to help anyone, you must help them make decisions that lead to actions.

I was able to succeed in school because people helped me make decisions that changed my actions and my habits. While walking alongside me, they helped me develop my decision muscles. That is, they helped me see that I had the power to make decisions that led to success. Eventually, I learned that little successes lead to bigger successes.

For example, teachers and coaches helped me decide to attend school two days in a row, then three, and then five. I eventually developed the habit of going to school every day. That habit started with a belief but was activated by a decision.

Although I did not become a decent student overnight, teachers convinced me to make the decision to turn in two homework assignments two days in a row. That decision to not only do my homework but also turn it in two days in a row strengthened my decision muscles. Those two assignments led to three, then four, and then five. I eventually developed the habit of doing my homework every night. I made a decision that led to action and better habits.

Even though I did not know how to write an essay, I decided to learn how to write an introduction, then a body, and then a conclusion. I eventually developed the habit of writing regularly. That habit started with me making a decision.

My decisions led to little successes, and my little successes led to bigger successes. Those successes helped me develop habits to help me to continue to succeed. My habits flowed from my actions, and my actions flowed from my decisions. Nothing changed until I made a decision. I share that with you so you can see that you have the power to help people make decisions that could help them take actions and develop habits that could drastically improve the quality of their lives.

I say all this to encourage you to help people make decisions. It is not enough to present solutions to people. It is not enough to convince them that they can succeed in school, work, or life. Rather, you have to ask them to make a decision to accept your proposal or recommendation. You have to do your best to help people make a decision.

If the man who reached me on that park bench had only told me what I needed to do, without asking me to make a decision to do it, I would have never returned to school. If my teacher in high school only told me that I needed to go to college without actually asking me to make a decision - a mental purchase- to go to college, then I am almost sure that I would not have gone to college when I did, if ever.

My life changed because they asked me to make a decision—to decide—to follow their advice. They placed the ball in my court. They put the responsibility on me to change my own life. The people who helped me most realized that they couldn't change me. All they could do was convince me to change myself. I think they realized that my only hope for making those changes was by making the decision to ownership of my life and my future.

Indeed, they took the last step involved in reaching me: People extended their HAND. The "H" in R.E.A.C.H. stands for hand. To reach someone, you have to reach out your hand figuratively, and sometimes literally, to ask for them to make a commitment. You must ask them to make a decision.

Now I want to share with you some practical ways to ask someone to make a decision or a commitment.

# THE STAIR-STEP

First, there is the Stair-Step. Some people have called it the ascending close. Others have called it the part-by-part close. I personally do not care what you name it. I care that you use it. The Stair-Step approach to reaching out your hand involves you organizing, and asking, a set of questions in ascending order that will cause the people with whom you are speaking to say "yes." For it to be effective, you need to organize your questions carefully and organize them in ascending order so that you can ultimately lead them to make a commitment.

So here is just an example of it:

"Do you want more out of life?" They better say yes.

"Do you want to be happy." Yes!

"Do you want to be fulfilled?" Yes!

"Do you want to be able to help a lot of people in your life?"

"Do you want to be successful? Yes!

"Do you want to make the most of your life?"

"Do you want better grades?" Yes

"Do you want a happy family?" Yes

"Do you want to be great?"

"Do you want to make a difference in the world?"

"Do you…" Yes! Yes! Yes!

You get the point.

Now you just keep asking these kinds of questions in ascending order. Then, when you feel that the person really means it, then you transition to the extension of your hand: "If I could show you how to do those things, would you be interested?" Yes!

"How soon would you want to get started?" RIGHT NOW!

Again, the idea is for you to ask several questions in ascending or-der—questions that you believe they will answer in the affirmative.

Then you ask them, "how soon would you like to get started?"

Write your questions down on paper, organize them in ascending order, placing the easiest "yeses" first. Then practice asking them. Rephrase them, play with them for a little while, until you feel comfortable with them; and then ask the young person to make a commitment.

# THE SANDWICH

Picture a sandwich. You have a piece of bread, you have something in the middle, and then you have another piece of bread.

When you are using The Sandwich, you're simply "sandwiching" the decision with benefits, benefit-decision-benefit. Okay, you have the decision in the middle of the two benefits. So let's say you have just laid out, you've just recommended that this kid take school seriously, that this kid picks up their grades. You've laid out an action plan.

To do so, you first start talking about the benefits with the young person. "You'll be able to pick up your grades; you'll be able to play on the team; you will be able to go on this field trip; you will be able to get X; now you'll be able to go to college…and yes you're going to have to work hard, but just think about the opportunities that could come. Think about the money you might be able to make. Think about the jobs that might be offered to you. Think about the business that you want to grow. Think about the people you will be able to help. Think about the best places you will be able to travel…"

Then you Reach out your hand: "Why don't you give it a try?" You sandwiched the cost between the benefits so that they focus on the rewards of what they will be getting as opposed to what they will be losing, or what it is going to cost them in terms of work.

# THE SCALE

You just ask, "on a scale of 1 to 10—ten being you are ready to make a commitment; one being you are nowhere near ready—on a scale of 1 to 10, where are you concerning being ready to make this decision?"

If they say anything other than 10, you simply say, "okay, you are at (# between 1–10) now; what would it take to get you to a 10?" Then, you just listen. Let them respond. Listen respectfully, and if their objections can be overcome, then respond appropriately. If you have responses to their objections, you can then Reach out your hand: "Obviously that concern you have is not as big as you think it is. So there is really nothing in the way of you making this commitment today. So why don't you give it a try? How soon can you get started?

# THE BEN FRANKLIN

You start by just asking, "you want to make the best decision possible, right?" They usually will say yes. Then you continue, "well, why don't we try something that Benjamin Franklin used to do when he needed to make a major decision?"

Then you explain, " Benjamin Franklin was an inventor. He was a millionaire and a Founding Father of the United States. Whenever he needed to make an important decision, he used to pull out a piece of paper, draw a line down the middle, creating two columns. In the top left column, he wrote down reasons he should take a course of action. On the top right column of that piece of paper, he wrote down reasons against making that course of action."

Then you ask your young person, "Why do not we give that a try?" Then you pull out your piece of paper, draw a line down the middle, and on the top left column, you write down "Reasons For." Then you ask the young person, "what are some reasons for you picking up your grades?" (or whatever). Then you help them make that list as long as possible. You want to help them write down the benefits of taking a specific course of action.

Then ask them, "Have we covered everything?" Once they say yes, then you slide the piece of paper over to them and say, "Now you come up with reasons against making this decision, or taking this course of action." More often than not, they will only be able to come up with two or three. In any case, YOU MUST NOT HELP THEM COME UP WITH REASONS AGAINST!

Let them come up with their reasons against making this decision. If the "Reasons For" list is really long and the Reasons Against" list is concise, you can then Reach out your hand: "well, it looks like you have made your decision. So how soon do we want to get started?"

## THE SECONDARY

This technique simply involves focusing on a minor part of your presentation. People use this on us all the time. If you are at a shoe store, and someone asks you, "would you like the size 8 or size 9?" If you respond to that question, they are assuming that you've made the purchase, and chances are that you have. You have made the purchase emotionally. When people use this approach, they are focusing on the secondary part of their presentation, never asking you if you are going to make the purchase; but which purchase you are going to make.

You can use this with the people you want to help—Reach out your hand: "Are you going to do your math first, or work on your essay?" You've started with the end, asking them which homework assignment they're going to work on.

# THE 3 QUESTIONS

Sometimes you can just ask them three questions: 1. Can you see where this could help you pick up your grades? 2. Are you really interested in picking up your grades? 3. If you were ever going to start picking up your grades, when do you think would be the best time to start?"

# THE NO

This is a short, simple one you can use. All you need to do is ask, "are there any questions that you have for me?" If they say "no, you pretty much covered everything," you have to assume that they have just made a purchase. So you just go ahead and act like they just said yes. You have to act like they just made a decision, it's the negative answer close. You Reach out your hand: "why don't you give it a try?

# THE PROMISE ME

A little while ago, I was being recruited by two different organizations. Both of them wanted me to come and work for them. One organization reached out to me, and they said, "man, we would really like you on our staff, we think you could make a tremendous difference here. You would have a great impact here. We just want you to come." Well, another organization was recruiting me at about the same time. And when I mentioned the first opportunity, they pulled me aside and said, "Before you make a decision to go with anyone else, would you please come and talk to me first?" They asked me to promise them.

How can you use that with the people you want to reach? Reach out your hand: "Hey listen, I know you are thinking about doing X, or I know you have the opportunity to do X, but do this for me:

before you make a decision, would you come back to me, and talk to me before you follow through with that decision? Would you do that for me, please?"

# THE WALK-AWAY

After you have made your strongest appeal to the person, but the young person is not being persuaded. So, in defeat, you shake their hand, and you say, "Thank you for your time, you know. I appreciate you. Thank you for hearing me out. I'll see you later." Then you walk away. And as you are walking away, you turn around, and you say, "you know what? Just before I go, can I ask you a question? I've done my best today, and I really, I really want to make a difference, and I feel like I just missed something; and, I don't want that to happen again in the future when I'm talking to someone else. Would you mind telling me why—what is the real reason you did not make the decision to accept what I recommended to you? Just shoot straight with me."

Then, if they oblige, and share something with you that you have an actual response to, go sit back down, and you try one last time to convince them to make a decision.

There are many more ways to reach out your hand. I've just given you a sample here. In this chapter, I just wanted to provide you with several ways you can ask someone to make a decision. But the key is, you have to ask them to make a decision, you have to reach out your hand- to convince them to make a commitment.

In every case, you have to appeal to their heart, you have to appeal to their minds, you have to lead with their needs by talking about the benefits, and then you need to ask them to make a decision.

I need to mention something about the difference between motivation and manipulation. You should never to try to manipulate people. Manipulation is when you try to get someone else to do something because it is going to benefit you. Motivation, however, is when you are trying to introduce something into people's lives to to help them. Motivation is when you have their best interests at heart, not yours. Don't try to manipulate people; try to motivate them. There is a big difference between the two. Manipulation benefits you; motivation benefits them. Are you trying to reach them so you look good, or are you trying to reach them so that their lives will improve? Motivation involves you trying to help people get better. You are trying to improve their personal circumstances. You are trying to give them a sense of joy, a sense of happiness, or a sense of purpose. To do that, you need to somehow make sure you are trying to motivate people rather than manipulate them.

Motivation is you trying to do something that is in the best interest of someone else. You get nothing more than a sense of gratitude for having helped them, and that is it. The real benefit is theirs. If that is not the case in your efforts, then you might be teetering on the edge of manipulation.

You have to have the best interests of others at heart. You have to be persuasive. You are selling ideas, you are selling hope, and you are selling change. So you have to do everything in your power to get people to make mental purchases, and you get people to make mental purchases by reaching out your hand!

If you reach out your hand, you can help change someone's life. If you reach out your hand, you can help them see their own infinite possibilities and leave their souls in joyous awe. If you reach out your hand, you can help change a family and an entire generation. If you reach out your hand, you can change the world!

So don't let crucial moments pass without you asking people you love to make a decision that could help them improve the quality of their lives. If you can see that they have become aware of an imbalance in their lives, then reach out your hand!

They might not make a purchase, mentally or emotionally on the spot, but at least you will have given them the chance to do so. Also, they will probably remember the feeling they had as a result of speaking with you.

After you have become culturally self-aware, you reach others by first building meaningful relationships with them. Second, you engage them by building bridges between their contexts and your content. Third, you must help them become painfully aware of the imbalances in their lives. Fourth, you must begin to convince them they can succeed by giving them glimpses of their own possibilities. Fifth, you must reach out your hand and walk with them, empower them, and to cheer for them. That is the R.E.A.C.H. approach. That is how you REACH others, and that is how you can help change someone's life.

A little while ago, I was speaking at a school in the Chicago area, and after my presentation was over, my host was rushing me to the exit doors so I could head to my next presentation at another school. But on my way out of the door, a custodian stopped me, "Mr. Scott! Please, we need your help." He then led me to a bathroom. The closer I got to the bathroom door, I could hear someone crying. I looked at the custodian, and asked him, "What's wrong?" "We don't know," he said, "but he won't talk to anyone." I walked into the bathroom and saw a tall young man bent over, sobbing. I eased over to him, and quietly asked, "Hey, buddy. My name is Manny Scott. What's wrong?"

He looked toward me, stood up, with tears pouring down his face. "Mr. Scott," he said, wiping his tears, "I was going home today to kill myself." I didn't say a word. I waited for him to keep talking.

"Two weeks ago, I walked into my living room, and I found my father hanging. My mother abandoned us a long time ago, and I don't know where she is…So I have no one. I have no one. The only person I had is now gone. I can't pay rent, I don't know where I'm going to go. I don't—I was going home today to kill myself."

I just stared, as he continued. "But as I was sneaking past the auditorium, to go home, I heard you speaking, and something told me to stop and listen. I felt compelled to listen. So for the whole presentation, I was in the back of the room, listening ... Mr. Scott, I didn't know there was anyone in the world who understood my pain. I didn't believe I could make it through this pain. I'm in here crying because you have given me a reason to keep living. You have helped me see that I can make it. That I need to keep living. That I am here for a reason. You helped me see that I can make it through the pain ... Mr. Scott," he looked me directly in my eyes, "thank you! Thank you for saving my life!"

I recently received a letter from that young man. He graduated from college and is now a counselor who helps traumatized people.

I share that with you not to impress you, but to impress upon you that REACH is changing people's lives all over the world.

If you apply the things I have shared with you in this book, test scores go up, people will sit at the edge of their seats to listen to you, people will look forward to seeing you, and people might even find you one day to thank you for helping them. If you work to REACH others, you will help them reach their potential.

So no matter how bleak the circumstances may seem, do not give up on people. Work to REACH them, for you might be the one per- son- the one person- to keep them from giving up. You might be the one person who prevents them from committing suicide, from picking up a gun or shooting up a school. REACH them.

As I prepare to end this book, I must to do what I have asked you to do for others- extend my hand to you.

My friend, I now extend my hand to you. Will you commit? Now that you have made it to the end of this book, what are you going to do? Will you close this book and return to doing things the way you have always done them? Will you go back to business-as-usual? Or, will you commit to doing something different, to trying something new? I hope that you renew your commitment to serve. I hope that you renew your commitment to speak, to teach, to coach, to lead, to help, to love with all your heart, soul, mind, and strength. Someone else's life and destiny are tied to your response. Please take my hand. Please accept this challenge. Please receive this commission, and go REACH others so they can REACH their potential!

# R.E.A.C.H.

# AFTERWORD

# SELF-CARE

In 2012, I had been on the road for about 300 days. I had spoken over 200 events and had invested my all into reaching people. I was serving, loving, and helping others in over 40 states and several countries. Then after my last event of the year, my wife and I walked to our hotel room. Once we entered our room, and the door closed behind us, I just started crying, and my hands were shaking. My wife asked me, "What's wrong?" I told her I did not know. I was on the edge of a nervous breakdown, and I didn't realize it until it was nearly too late.

Friend, trying to reach others can be exhausting work. It can get so difficult that it takes you to the edge of your capacity. Also, if you do not take care of yourself, you could end up like me, and put yourself at risk of having a nervous breakdown.

I share this to encourage you to keep first things first in your life. Take care of yourself. Exercise regularly and eat healthy foods. Get eight to nine hours of sleep at night. Take vacations as often as you need them. Go sit in a park or on a beach somewhere, and recharge. Soak in some bathwater and read a good book.

Finally, enjoy your loved ones, your family, and your friends. If you are married or have a family, make sure that you do not neglect your family in your quest to reach others. Yes, there are times when our families have to sacrifice their time with us for a greater good, but what good is to save the whole world and lose your family?

In any case, thank you for your desire to make a difference in the lives of others. I am so glad we are on the same team.

—Manny

# R.E.A.C.H.

# ABOUT THE AUTHOR

Manny Scott is the founder of Ink International, Inc., an education consulting firm focused on empowering individuals to improve their lives and the lives of those around them, helping increase student achievement and leader effectiveness, and helping prevent dropouts and suicides. An original Freedom Writer, whose story is told in part in the movie Freedom Writers, Manny speaks at conferences, conventions and schools worldwide. He is the author of *Your Next Chapter*, *R.E.A.C.H.*, *Speak!*, *Even on Your Worst Day You can Be a Student's Best Hope*, and *Turning the Page*, his memoir. He has energized more than two million leaders, educators, volunteers, and students worldwide with his authentic, inspiring messages of hope. You may reach him at info@MannyScott.com.

**FOR MORE INFO AND RESOURCES, CONTACT US AT:**
Ink International
P.O. Box 464868
Lawrenceville, GA 30042
Phone: (888) 987-TURN

Or visit our website at:
**www.MannyScott.com**

Made in the USA
Columbia, SC
15 February 2020

87860758R00124